Thine Is the Power

Thine Is the Power

Lance Lambert

LANCE LAMBERT MINISTRIES

Richmond, VA

ISBN 978-1-68389-038-6
www.lancelambert.org

Contents

Preface

During June, 1992 at the Christian Family Conference in Richmond, Virginia, Lance Lambert spoke four messages on Thine is the Power! These messages have been transcribed into this book. The spoken form has been preserved and only necessary editing done for clarity.

1.
The Power Belongs to God

Matthew 6:13b (KJV)

For thine is the kingdom, and the power, and the glory, for ever. Amen.

1 Chronicles 29:10–14

Wherefore David blessed [the Lord] before all the assembly; and David said, Blessed be thou, O [Lord], the God of Israel our father, for ever and ever. Thine, O [Lord], is the greatness, and the power, and the glory, and the victory, and the majesty: for all that is in the heavens and in the earth is thine; thine is the kingdom, O [Lord], and thou art exalted as head above all. Both riches and honor come of thee, and thou rulest over all; and in thy hand is power and might; and in thy hand it is to make great, and to give strength unto all. Now therefore, our God, we thank thee, and praise thy glorious name. But who am I, and what is my people, that we should be able to offer so willingly after this sort? for all things come of thee, and of thine own have we given thee.

Psalm 62:11–12

God hath spoken once, Twice have I heard this, That power belongeth unto God. Also unto thee, O Lord, belongeth lovingkindness [steadfast love]; For thou renderest to every man—according to his work.

"Thine is the kingdom, and the power, and the glory, for ever and ever." We are going to consider the power that is mentioned in this Scripture: "Thine is the power." The Lord quite deliberately put the power in the centre because there is no point in a kingdom without power. It can neither be built nor maintained nor fulfilled in any way without the power of God. Nor can we ever know the glory of God covering the earth as the waters cover the sea unless we experience the power of God. It is God who, in the end, has to so wonderfully fulfil His purpose that the glory of God can come. So in many ways, practically, this matter of power is pivotal; it is central to the whole matter. That is why we do not say, "Thine is the power, and the kingdom, and the glory," or "Thine is the glory, and the kingdom, and the power." We say, "Thine is the kingdom, and the power, and the glory."

There are a number of words that are translated by this English word power. In Hebrew, we have a whole number of words which are translated by this one English word power. There are two particular words in Hebrew that are used and both have the same idea, although slightly different. But I think it best for us to keep to the English. The Greek has a number of words translated by this English word power. There are two principal words in Greek that are used, but again, they basically have the same idea of ability: "to be able to do something, ability to do something, to make something possible—strength, might, power."

Thine Is the Power

As we consider this whole question of power, I want first to underline the very simple fact, which is fundamental but absolutely essential to our understanding of this whole matter of God's power, that all true power belongs to God. Apart from God, there is no power. We find this in the prayer the Lord taught us to pray: "Thine is the power." We read it again in that great declaration of King David: "Thine is the power. In Thy hand is power and might." Even King Jehoshaphat said the same thing: "Power belongs to You" (see II Chronicles 20:6). The Psalmist said, "Once has God spoken, twice have I heard this; power belongs to the Lord" (see Psalm 62:11).

It comes as a great shock to some believers to know that all power is of God. For myself, there is a tremendous encouragement and comfort in understanding this, but I recognize for some Christians it brings a lot of theological or philosophical problems. The fact of the matter is that no despot, no dictator can rule apart from the power of God. Even unsaved, demonized rulers can only rule as long as God gives them breath. They have no power apart from God. If God says one word, they will drop dead at that moment. I remember years ago when Mao Tse-tung swam the Yellow River to prove something—if, in fact, he ever did it.

But suppose he did swim the Yellow River. What did it prove? Only that God gave him the power. God could have given him a heart attack a third of the way across. It is so silly when you think about it, yet we all are so afraid of these evil powers. We feel that as long as we have someone righteous and good in charge, which is understandable, everything will be all right; but in actual fact, everything is determined by God. The rise of Marxism was determined by God, the duration of Marxism was determined by God, and its collapse and fall was determined by God. Everything comes and everything goes, and only the Lord is forever. That is why we say, "Thine is the power." I realize again that this gives us quite a lot of problems, but we need to understand that altogether apart from good men and decent men and, of course above all, saved men ruling by the power of God, dictators rule by the power of God and so do despots. Even more shocking is that Satan himself only has power in so far as God gives it to him. I know that some people have problems with this; but since we are talking about this whole matter of power, we have to deal with it.

These are the words of our Lord Jesus spoken to Pontius Pilate, who represented the whole might and power of Rome: "Thou wouldest have no power against me, except it were given thee from above: therefore, he that delivered me unto thee hath greater sin" (John 19:11). Now most Christians would not think of Pontius Pilate being able, by the power of God, to do what he did, yet Jesus said, "You have no power unless God gives it to you."

Then we have the apostle Paul speaking by the Holy Spirit in Romans 13:1–2: "Let every soul be in subjection to the higher powers: for there is no power but of God; and the powers that be are ordained of God. Therefore he that resisteth the power, withstandeth the ordinance of God: and they that withstand shall receive to themselves judgment."

Notice again these words: "There is no power but of God." But of whom was the apostle Paul speaking? He was speaking of the Roman authorities. He was speaking of those who were absolutely pagan—without God, without Christ, and without hope; and in many cases, demonized. The imperial kaiser, the Roman Kaiser actually believed that he was God manifest; yet Paul said, "You must be subject to these authorities, because they cannot rule apart from God." Now the fact that they do rule apart from God is interesting. They do not rule consciously by the power of God. They are not under the direction of the Lord. They do not hear the Lord. They are not actually obeying the word of God. But the fact still remains their life is totally determined by God's will, and the moment the Lord says, "That is it," it is it; they are finished. They cannot live one single minute beyond the power of God given to them.

Some will say, "What has this got to do with us? We are believers; we love the Lord Jesus; we want to know the power of God in our lives." We are moving into tremendous days when more and more evil is going to be manifested, when demonized world leaders will rise, when we will have a demonized world government and a demonized new world order. We do not know how long we will have to go into that before the Lord appears to take us. But the fact remains, that if you and I are not able to see beyond them to the Lord, we shall never be able to overcome. We have got to be able to see beyond fallen flesh and blood, beyond demonized and Satanized flesh and blood to the Lord Himself. One old divine imagined Paul saying to the soldier when Paul was in chains:

"I have more right to be on this end of the chain than you have to be on that end." It was the Lord who Paul said had chained him. He was not ashamed of those chains. They were, in some way, his glory because he had seen beyond the limitation of his physical freedom, beyond the circumstances that were so difficult to the Lord whose power was manifest. The most amazing thing about the apostle Paul is that in those circumstances, with those chains, with a soldier chained to him in everything to do with his life for a number of years, he was used by God to write some of the foundational letters of the Bible. We would have thought he should have been sent away to a great retreat on some great mountain top in glorious surroundings, being served by the saints. Instead, he was surrounded by soldiers who did not know God, some of them probably brutalized soldiers, demonic in many ways, under the authority of a demonized emperor. In those circumstances, he fulfilled his ministry; he finished his course; he kept the faith. I say that is tremendous! Sometimes we say, "Thine is the power," and it does not mean anything; it is a phrase. But if Paul ever repeated those words, it came from the heart out of reality: "Thine is the kingdom, and the power, and the glory, for ever.

"And then shall be revealed the lawless one (who has already been described as the man of sin and the son of perdition), whom the Lord Jesus shall slay with the breath of his mouth, and bring to nought by the manifestation of his coming; even he, whose coming is according to the working of Satan with all power and signs and lying wonders, and with all deceit of unrighteousness" (II Thessalonians 2:8–10a).

I find it so wonderful that the Lord Jesus will just breathe on this monolith of a man, this gigantic man, this antichrist, this man of sin, and he will shrivel. He will bring to nought all his great systems, his world-wide new order, 666, and all that. He will bring that awful beast and the other beast and the whole thing to an end by just breathing on them. I do not know why Christians get frightened. As long as that one reigns, it is by the power of God; it is within the will of God. And when the Lord says, "That is enough," it will be enough. The Lord will simply breathe on him. The Lord will not have to get up steam, if I may put it so irreverently, and work up some great rocket-propelling judgment upon him, shooting something, one after the other, at him. All the Lord will have to do is breathe on him and he will be finished. Such is the power of God! Oh, the infinite power of God! the sovereign power of God! the creative power of God! the invincible power of God! God's power is infinite. There is nothing beyond it. There is nothing that compromises Him; there is nothing that limits Him. With God, nothing is impossible. It is marvellous.

The Lord does not always do everything we want, but He actually can do anything. It is so wonderful just to contemplate for a few moments His infinite power. Who else is infinite in power? Some think you have God here who has power and Satan there who has power. The two are locked in a battle and it is a question of who is going to win. We think the Lord has an edge over Satan, but Satan is nothing compared with God. Satan is not infinite; he is finite. He may have enormous power, enormous ability, enormous intelligence, greater than all of us put together, but the fact still remains that he is a created being. He is not equal to God. He may think because of his pride that he is, but he is not. God is infinite; Satan is finite. God is uncreated; Satan is created.

When we think about this and the power of God, no wonder we can say from the heart: "Thine is the power." Is there anything too hard for the Lord? Is there anything the Lord cannot do? Is there any problem the Lord cannot solve? Is there any knot he cannot untie? Is there any obstacle he cannot overcome? Is there any contradiction he cannot remove? His power is infinite.

Think of how sovereign the Lord is. He does not get agitated; He does not get neurotic; He does not get into a great panic. He who sits in the heavens will laugh. Oh, I love it! Some Christians cannot imagine God laughing; but if God put laughter in our souls, He must at times have a laugh Himself, since we are the palest reflection of Him. In Psalm 2, when the whole world is upside down like a turbulent sea and a huge typhoon is sweeping everything before it and all the people are crying out and saying, "Away with God, and away with His Messiah," we think the Lord would be very nervous with what is happening. The whole universe is upside down; Satan is energizing them; and all the Lord does is sit. He does not even get up.

"He that sitteth in the heavens." Why is He sitting? He is sitting on the throne. He is sovereign. This is not going to do anything to His sovereignty. He is not perturbed; He is not panicked; He is not dismayed; He does not even feel that He is contradicted.

"He that sitteth in the heavens will laugh: the Lord will have them in derision. Yet I have set my King upon my holy hill of Zion" (Psalm 2:4, 6). "I have My King in the right place in spite of all this. Let them do their war dances; let them say what they want to say; let them contradict Me; let them seek to frustrate Me. The very power that they are using to do it is from Me, and all I have to do is say the word and it will be the end of them all."

Creative Power

"Thine is the power." It is creative power. It says in Luke 1:37, "For no word from God shall be void of power." When the Lord speaks, He does not do what some of us do sometimes, using words as a kind of rhetoric, merely for effect. When the Lord speaks, there is power within every word. We think of Shakespeare as genius, and rightly so. We think of many others as genius, and rightly so; but no word of theirs has ever delivered an alcoholic from his alcoholism or a drug addict from his drug addiction, or healed a broken home, or healed a broken heart. Yet one word from God brought by the Spirit into a human life can change the whole course of that life. It can bring healing; it can bring deliverance. It is amazing what God can do through His word. It is creative.

"For the word of God is living and active." It is creative. God spoke, and suddenly, there was a universe. One word—"Let there be light"—and there was light. "Let the heavens and the earth be parted by a firmament"—and it happened. I am not saying how it happened. I know there is all this talk about evolution. There may be some kind of evolutionary process within certain species, but I believe Darwin is utterly wrong. The fact remains that not in one place but in many places throughout the old covenant as well as the new, God's word says: "By His word, He created the heavens and the earth." If you want to understand the power of God, then remember that by a word He created out of nothing the things that are. Oh, the power of God!

Invincible Power

God's power is invincible. The very fact that He lets Satan have his way and then uses him is amazing. The most amazing thing of all is that God uses the powers of darkness and demonic activity to perfect the saints for Himself. You would think that Satan would realize that and he would say, "Every time I do anything, it turns out for good for those people." But pride is an unbelievable thing; it blinds us. Anyone who is a genuinely proud person is a blind person on certain issues that touch their own self-centeredness. They will not see and cannot see. They are totally blind because of pride. I think that is very true of Satan.

All power belongs to God. His power is invincible. What God has purposed, God will fulfil. It may take Him quite a time as far as we who are living in time and space are concerned; but the fact of the matter is that in the end, He will achieve that which He set out to do. He will not leave a hoof or a horn to Satan.

Take again this matter of the word of God, which I think is so important, especially in this generation and the days that lie ahead:

"For this they wilfully forget, that there were heavens from of old, and an earth compacted out of water and amidst water, by the word of God; by which means the world that then was, being overflowed with water, perished: but the heavens that now are, and the earth, by the same word have been stored up for fire, being reserved against the day of judgment and destruction of ungodly men." II Peter 3:5–7

"By faith we understand that the worlds have been framed by the word of God, so that what is seen hath not been made out of things which appear." Hebrews 11:3

"Who (speaking of the Lord Jesus) being the effulgence of his glory, and the very image of his substance, and upholding all things by the word of his power." Hebrews 1:3a

You will notice it is all by the word of God. It is endless when you think of the word of God; and you have the word of God in your hands. It is unbelievable to think that by this word of God, He created all things and upholds all things.

Salvation Power

Another wonderful thing that is said in I Peter is that we are begotten again by the word of God (see I Peter 1:23). We are born of God's word.

"Let the word of Christ dwell in you richly," (Colossians 3:16). James speaks of receiving the implanted word because this word, which is living and active and can divide between soul and spirit, is absolutely essential if you and I are going to be delivered from the works of darkness and really conformed to the image of God's Son.

All power belongs to God in creation; He created the world, and in the end, He will fulfil His purpose for this old earth. In the end, there will be a new heaven and a new earth, wherein dwells righteousness, by the word of God. In salvation, Christ is the power of God. It was through the Lord Jesus that all things that were created were created. We know that it was for Him; and in Him, it all holds together. Where would you and I be except for the salvation that is in the Lord Jesus? Christ crucified is the power of God. There is no salvation outside of the Lord Jesus. There are mountains of religion, but only in the Lord Jesus is there salvation. There can be no transformation apart from Christ as the power of God. The Holy Spirit is the One who brings into us all the life and nature and qualities of the Lord Jesus and begins to reproduce them and change us into His likeness.

The Power of the Fallen Man

Babylon

We shall never understand this subject fully unless we realize the power of fallen man. Babylon is the illustration and exemplification of fallen man's power. Man energized by Satan, man inspired by demons is Babylon. Don't get into your head that Babylon was some horrific place that would absolutely appall you. If you could have gone on a tour of Babylon some three thousand or more years ago, you would have been absolutely bowled over by the magnificence of Babylon. If you had lived in that day, you never would have seen anything like it with its avenues and boulevards, its hanging gardens, its zoological gardens, its stock exchange, its postal system, its marvellous temples, its iron gates, and its huge sea canals bringing ships right up from the Persian Gulf into the heart of the capital. It took three days to walk across greater Babylon. It was magnificent with its parks and gardens, its institutions, and everything else.

It all began in Genesis 11. "And they said, Come, let us build us a city, and a tower, whose top may reach unto heaven, and let us make us a name; lest we be scattered abroad upon the face of the whole earth" (Genesis 11:4). Notice what they said: "Let us make us a name." That is the heart of Babylon.

Here is the second thing: "Lest we be scattered abroad." In other words, let us do something for our security and self-preservation. There is yet another thing: "Let us build a tower whose top will reach to the heavens." Whatever they meant by this tower, the idea was to bridge heaven and earth—to bring heaven on earth and earth to heaven. Was it the first skyscraper? We do not know. Was it the first space exploration attempt? We do not know. Was it merely astrological, occult? We do not fully know. All we know is that fallen man, energized by demons, had in his head, somehow or other, to unite heaven with earth without God. By their own abilities, by their own gifts, by their own talents, by their own energies, by their own ingenuity, without God, without God's Messiah, somehow or other, they were going to bridge the gulf between heaven and earth and earth and heaven. They were inspired by the idea that they would make for themselves a name which would last forever.

In chapter 10 of Genesis, you find there was a certain man whose name was Nimrod. He was called a mighty one and a powerful one. He was a man of power. Then it says he was a mighty hunter. He founded Babylon. He was a powerful man: "Let us make us a name lest we be scattered abroad; let us build a tower that will reach heaven." Do you know that man has been doing that ever since? That is the description of man's power, man's energies, man's glory. Babylon was the flowering of it. It was so magnificent.

He called it *Bab-il* which means in Aramaic, "the gate of God." He said the thing he was building was the gateway into a golden age, the gateway into a new order, the gateway into a new, glorious age of prosperity and equality. Bab-il is the gate of God without God. It is what men have created. Oh, there are plenty of gods in it, but they are all projections of man's own mind and heart. You will find every form of religion that you wish within this Babylon, but it is not the true and living God, nor does it have any relationship to the Messiah of the true and living God.

It does not tell us in the word, but somewhere God must have said to some Jewish scribe: "Don't call it Bab-il; it is not Bab-il. You call it Babel. *Babel* means "confusion." So what fallen man in all his power calls the gate of God, God calls confusion. If you look at the whole of human history from that day onward to now, that is its epitaph. Every new empire, every new superpower, every new philosophy, every new ideology is called by man a gate of God, a divine gateway into a new era, into a new order, into a new world with a new man. God has said it is nothing but confusion. It does not have foundations; it cannot last.

I have often likened Babylon to Washington with all those magnificent buildings. You can stand by the Washington Monument and look right down to the Lincoln Memorial and across to the Jefferson Memorial and across to the White House and then up to the Capitol. There is the Supreme Court building and the Library building. I think they are wonderful, all in the classical style. You can see the beauty of the symmetry, the beauty of the design and the architecture.

As you are in Babylon, looking around at the magnificent city with its avenues and moving traffic and all the life of a great capital city, some Jewish prophet is standing over there and saying, "All this is going to disappear."

"Disappear? Where did he come from?"

"Jerusalem."

"Jerusalem! That little, old town of only five hundred thousand people, buried it could slide down by an earthquake into the Jordan Valley. It has no avenues, no boulevards, no canals. It has no magnificent buildings, as such. Tell him his Jerusalem is going to disappear."

"No," he says, "this great metropolis will disappear so completely that shepherds will take flocks across it and not even know that beneath their feet lies this great city."

It is exactly what happened. They used to talk of Babylon at the beginning of the last century as a legend like Atlantis and said it never existed. It was the German critics who said it, but it was a German archaeologist who discovered it. Isn't it wonderful—the Lord's power? It was a German archaeologist who discovered Babylon under the sands. When they began to uncover it and uncover it, we began to realize that Babylon was far more magnificent than even the Bible describes it; and yet it all disappeared.

Nevertheless, Babylon has become the symbol of everything. Egypt in all its glory, Greece in all its glory, Persia in all its glory, Rome in all its glory—it is all Babylon. Today, modern civilization, even though it is supposed to have so much Christianity at its roots, is actually Babylon. It does not matter whether it is Washington or London or Paris or Moscow or Beijing, it is Babylon. It is man's glory, man's power, his ingenuity, his creative genius, everything that is the consequence of his talents and his gifts. The whole thing is: "We will make a name for ourselves"—whether it is Babylon, Egypt, Persia, Greece, Rome, or modern civilization.

We are right on the brink of a new thing happening: "We will make a name for ourselves, lest we be scattered abroad. We have to do this for our self-preservation—the preservation of mankind, the preservation of our civilization, the preservation of all that we have produced." They are trying, always, to unite heaven to earth without the living God and without His Messiah. Oh, they will take the name of Christ but not the Lord Jesus. They will take phrases from the word of God but not the word of the living God. They will use it as a facade in a mishmash of world religions, in an apostate church, in a new world order; but it is Babylon. It is the power of man.

We are the witnesses in our day and generation of the rising up of the renewed Roman Empire, as incredible, as unbelievable as it may seem. Within the old world, within Europe has arisen a huge, monolithic, coming superpower of 361 million people with the greatest resources of the world and the greatest wealth behind them. It stretches from Iceland to Portugal, from Ireland to Greece. In the end, it will take in the north African countries, which has already been decided, and even little Israel and Turkey. It is incredible that a Jewish prophet 2500 years ago saw it all. He said it would happen. Another Jewish apostle on the isle of Patmos saw it in even more clearly defined terms; it is described in Revelations 13. He saw the whole thing that we are seeing. Now some people have said that it would be the revival of the Holy Roman Empire. It is the most unbelievable thing. Nobody could have believed that after four to five hundred years of division, of wars that have grown into world wars, suddenly, within this very same area that saw the great Roman Empire all centred in Rome and later the Christianized Roman Empire centred in Rome, that now we would see this mammoth thing rising. Every single new member has to sign the treaty of Rome. In Europe, there has to be a world order or there will be a trade war that will tear the North American Continent to pieces.

Maybe you get afraid of these things, but why do you think God put it in the word? Of course, it is not to frighten us. He put it in the word that we might be encouraged. The Lord is coming, and the very power behind this whole thing is God's power. They are misusing it, make no mistake about it. They do not even recognize that it is God's power that allows this whole thing to come.

That is why I have said repeatedly that the United States has begun its decline. This does not mean that if God's people would only seek the Lord to do something spiritually in the American and Canadian people, He will not do it. He will do it. There could be an awakening and a revival of the most unbelievable power and dimension if God's people would only seek Him. But my knowledge of American church life leaves me very saddened. They are more interested in their beautiful buildings, their choirs, their ministerial offices, and all that kind of routine than in getting on their knees and repenting before the living God and seeking Him with all their heart.

As surely as I stand here, there is a new world order coming. A new-age religion is coming. An apostate church is coming, and the whole thing is the power of man. They call it a new age, but it is not. It is the old age. They call it a new world order; it is not. It is an old world order. They call it a new man; it is not. It is the old man.

It is the whole principle of Babylon coming to its climax, coming to its fruition, coming to its flowering, coming to its harvest. That is why we have to understand that nothing can reach God's end if it does not begin with God. All that I have talked about is still within the power of God, although it is man's power. When God wants to, He will bring it to an end.

Isn't it marvellous in the book of Revelation, however you interpret the book of Revelation, that when you go through it with all its beasts, persecution, martyrdom, the believers being hounded to the ends of the earth, the church being lukewarm and the Lord wanting to vomit it out of His mouth, 666 and all that, dragons, serpents, and everything at the end when Babylon seems to have reached her glory and her climax, then the whole thing falls in one day? I do not know if that day is symbolic or if it is an actual day, but in one day it falls (see Revelation 17–18). Then we hear the most unbelievable paean of worship in the heavens. It is almost (if I may put it with my dreadful imagination) as if all those saints and angels are hanging over the banister and the balustrades of heaven and crying, "Hallelujah!" There is so much beauty in Babylon, so much art in Babylon, so much magnificence in Babylon, so much good in Babylon; there are so many wonderful things in Babylon. Why are all those saints saying, "Hallelujah, hallelujah, the Lord has judged Babylon. He has destroyed it"? Then we hear those wonderful words: "Hallelujah, for the Lord our God, the Almighty reigneth. Let us rejoice and be exceeding glad, and let us give the glory unto him: for the marriage of the Lamb is come, and his wife hath made herself ready" (Revelation 19:6b–7). In the midst of this terrible Babylon coming to its climax, something is happening by the power of God. Something is happening within the nations. Something is happening on this earth, in spite of all Satan's power and energy and this kingdom of fallen man. The bride is making herself ready.

To Reach God's End, We Must Begin with God

I do not want to leave you with just this picture of the greatness of Babylon and all the rest of it. I want to say this: Origin is vital if God's end is to be reached. What begins with God can end with God, but what never begins with God can never end with God. Let me put it another way: If you begin with the Lord Jesus, you have every possibility of coming to God's end.

Psalm 87 speaks of some amazing things: "Glorious things are spoken of thee, O city of God." Then the psalmist goes on to tell of those that are born in that city, and he speaks, strangely enough, of Babylon, Philista, Egypt, Tyre, and all the peoples. Although they are living all over the place, that is not the point; they have been born in Jerusalem. You may be living here in the States; we may be living in all parts of the earth, but do we have a spiritual birth recorded in Jerusalem? That little Psalm ends with an extraordinary word which some liberal scholars say got attached to it because it does not seem to have anything to do with the Psalm: "All my springs are in thee." "Springs, fountains, sources, origins are all in you. It is all in you." Are we of Babylon or are we of Jerusalem? Is the Jerusalem that is above our mother? Are we born of the Spirit of God?

What is flesh is flesh. You can dress it up; you can christen it; you can baptize it; you can give it communion; you can put it on a church roll; you can put a dog collar on it; you can put a reverend in front of its name; you can put titles after its name; you can even get it to a cardinal, a bishop or even the pope; but it will not get into the kingdom if it is not born of God. We have to be born of God; we have to begin with the Lord. If we begin with the Lord, there is all the glorious possibility that God, by His grace, through His power, will bring us to the throne. I am not talking about salvation. Once you are saved, I believe you are saved; but I am talking about coming to the end that God has. He wants to bring us to the throne; He wants to bring us to be a part of the bride. In some glorious way, He wants to do a work in us that will make us part of His eternal government.

When you come to the last book of the Bible, at the very beginning, it is the Lord God Almighty who speaks: "I am the Alpha and the Omega, saith the Lord God, who is and who was and who is to come, the Almighty" (Revelation 1:8). But when we come to the end of the book of Revelation, in chapters 21 and 22, twice we have the same word: Jesus says, "I am the Alpha and Omega, the first and the last, the beginning and the end." Why is this message in the last book? It is because the Lord is saying that everything that begins with God is through the Lord Jesus. It has to be through the Lord Jesus, and only by the Lord Jesus can we come to God's end.

The book of Revelation gives us a very clear understanding of the end of everything. However glorious it may seem, whatever facade it has, we see its end. But those that begin with the Lord Jesus and continue with the Lord Jesus are found with the Lamb on Mount Zion. We see them coming down out of heaven, having the glory of God. Something marvellous has happened. That is why we are taught in that pattern prayer of our Lord Jesus to pray: "For thine is the kingdom, and the power, and the glory, for ever. Amen."

2.
The Exceeding Greatness of His Power

Ephesians 1:15–23

For this cause I also, having heard of the faith in the Lord Jesus which is among you, and the love which ye [have] toward all the saints, cease not to give thanks for you, making mention of you in my prayers; that the God of our Lord Jesus Christ, the Father of glory, may give unto you a spirit of wisdom and revelation in the knowledge of him; having the eyes of your heart enlightened, that ye may know what is the hope of his calling, what the riches of the glory of his inheritance in the saints, and what the exceeding greatness of his power to usward who believe, according to that working of the strength of his might which he wrought in Christ, when he raised him from the dead, and made him to sit at his right hand in the heavenly places, far above all rule, and authority, and power, and dominion, and every name that is named, not only in this world, but also in that which is to come: and he put all things in subjection under his feet, and gave him to be head over all things to the church, which is his body, the fulness of him that filleth all in all.

Ephesians 3:14–21
For this cause I bow my knees unto the Father, from whom every family in heaven and on earth is named, that he would grant you, according to the riches of his glory, that ye may be strengthened with power through his Spirit in the inward man; that Christ may dwell in your hearts through faith; to the end that ye, being rooted and grounded in love, may be strong to apprehend with all the saints what is the breadth and length and height and depth, and to know the love of Christ which passeth knowledge, that ye may be filled unto all the fulness of God. Now unto him that is able to do exceeding abundantly above all that we ask or think, according to the power that worketh in us, unto him be the glory in the church and in Christ Jesus unto all generations for ever and ever. Amen.

Philippians 3:10
That I may know him, and the power of his resurrection, and the fellowship of his sufferings, [being made conformable] unto his death.

In the last book of the sixty-six books that make up our Bible, the canon of Scripture, there is an almost unique phrase that comes in Revelation 1:8, 21:6, and 22:13. In Revelation 1:8 it is the Lord God Almighty who speaks: "I am the Alpha and the Omega, saith the Lord God, who is and who was and who is to come, the Almighty." In Revelation 21:6 it is the Lord Jesus who is speaking, and He says, "I am the Alpha and the Omega, the beginning and the end." When we come to chapter 22:13, it is the Lord Jesus speaking again, almost the very last words of the Bible: "I am the Alpha and the Omega, the first and the last, the beginning and the end." It is almost as if the whole, practical relevance of the Bible is summed up in these words. If you and I are going to reach God's end, we must begin with God's beginning. We cannot come to God's end if we do not begin with His beginning. God is the beginning and the end of everything as far as His kingdom is concerned, as far as His purpose is concerned. All the fulness of God is found in the Lord Jesus. So when it comes down to practical, relevant terms, it is finding the Lord Jesus and beginning with Him.

The Lord Jesus put it very simply: "That which is born of the flesh is flesh." You can dress it up; you can make it religious; you can Christianize it; you can baptize it; you can christen it; you can give it communion; you can put it on a church roll; you can dress it up in robes; you can put a title in front of it; you can do a thousand and one things to it, but it is still flesh. And it remains flesh. Only that which is born of the Spirit is spirit; therefore, only that which begins with the Lord Jesus can end with the Lord Jesus. This is a lesson that most believers learn very hardly, because somehow, even when we begin with the Lord Jesus, we begin to bring in things that do not have their source in the Lord Jesus. It is our energy, our strength, our gifts, our talents, everything to do with ourselves, the ways of this world, and the wisdom of this world.

Look at the mess we have made of the church. It is not that we are not the church, if we are born of God; but as soon as we come together, we make a mess of the whole thing because we begin, as it were, to use all the methods of the world. We turn it into a club like the rest of the world's clubs. We turn it into a society like the rest of the world's societies. We turn it into an institution like the rest of the world's institutions. Once that happens, God's end cannot be reached.

When the apostle talks about the exceeding greatness of His power to us-ward who believe, he almost exhausts human language. When we read the first chapter of Ephesians, it is almost as if human language is strained to its capacity to communicate what is ours in God, what is ours through the Lord Jesus. It is so tremendous.

It is almost as if while he was dictating the letter he suddenly said to the secretary or whoever was writing it down: "Should I tell them what I am praying? I am so afraid all this is going to be material for Bible studies, a kind of doctrine for theological seminaries, material for books to be written on to titillate Christians minds."

The secretary probably said to him, "I think it is a good idea if we tell them what we are praying."

The apostle Paul said, "I want you to know that I am praying not that you will mentally understand or appreciate or study just with the intellect what I am saying, but that the God and Father of our Lord Jesus, the Messiah, the Father of glory may grant to you a spirit of wisdom; that is, what to do with the knowledge, how to apply the knowledge. May He give you a spirit of wisdom and revelation, illumination, enlightenment, that you may know Him—not know about Him." Christians know all about the Lord, but it is knowing the Lord that counts. "That you may know him, the eyes of your heart being enlightened, that you may know what is the hope of his calling, what the riches of the glory of his inheritance in the saints, and what the exceeding greatness of his power to us-ward who believe." What else could he say? How else could he put it? He uses words that are almost extravagant, not because he is being extravagant but because he cannot put into human language the exceeding might, the exceeding power, the enormous magnitude of the power that God has made available to the child of God. If you and I only knew....

We can understand a little about the hope of our calling; we can even understand something about the riches of the glory of His inheritance in the saints, but then we do not have the power for anything to happen. It is all trapped in our mind. We can come to these conferences year after year, and our heads become bigger and bigger. I do not mean it in an unkind way, but we just become encyclopedic. We begin to plow into these things and study these things and talk about these things; but unless we know what the exceeding greatness of His power to us-ward who believe is, we shall never enter in practically to what is ours in the Lord. We shall never, as it were, become educated, prepared, trained for the hope of His calling. We shall never be able to become, practically, His inheritance.

"What the exceeding greatness of his power to us-ward who believe, according to that working of the strength of his might which he wrought in Christ, when he raised him from the dead" (Ephesians 1:19–20a).

There are so many superlatives here, so much that is tremendous, that somehow or other it begins to run off us like water off a duck's back; we cannot take it in.

"According to the [effective, effectual] working of the strength of God's might which He displayed in raising Jesus from the dead."

When the Lord Jesus finally became sin for us, when He died in our place, don't you think that Satan, having been blinded by pride as he is, mobilized all the forces of hell to keep Him dead? We know that it was impossible, but pride is of such a nature that Satan thought it might be possible to get hold of Him and keep Him in the tomb. I believe the word went out to all the hellish forces, and all the satanic powers of darkness mobilized: "Everything will be lost if He comes out of the tomb. He has finished the work of their salvation; but He needs to be alive if they, practically, are going to know what it is be saved." Romans says, "How much more will we be saved by His life." Oh, the power that God displayed, that God exercised.

Most of us have never had a visit from Satan. That is something we can thank God for. Most of us have had visits from minions in the highest satanic hierarchy, but very much lower down; and isn't that bad enough? Do any of you know anything about an hour of darkness, a day when there was a crisis in your life, when everything seemed to be given over to Satan, when it seemed as if the powers of evil came in like a flood? You felt so helpless, so weak. You felt as if everything was mobilized against you, making it impossible to come through. Can you imagine what it was like when Satan mobilized all his forces, all the powers of evil and darkness to keep Jesus in the tomb? Thank God, God raised Jesus from the dead and shattered, once and for all, the power of Satan. "Cast him out," as Jesus said. In that moment, he was shattered.

"To this end was the Son of God manifested, that he might destroy the works of the devil." 1 John 3:8b

"Since then the children are sharers in flesh and blood, he also himself in like manner partook of the same; that through death he might bring to nought him that had the power of death, that is, the devil; (and here is the resurrection) and might deliver all them who through fear of death were all their lifetime subject to bondage." Hebrews 2:15

The Lord Jesus was manifested to destroy the works of the devil. Oh, what works the devil has done! You don't have to look around in society; you don't have to look around in the world. You only have to look inside your own life, inside your own circumstances, very often inside your own family tree to find it all there. It is the works of the devil, the works of darkness, and Jesus was manifested to destroy the works of the devil. Think of this: God has brought to zero the power and authority of Satan. Zero is zero; it does not matter how many times you multiply it; it is still zero. When Jesus died on the cross, He brought to zero the power and authority of Satan. He zeroed him; he nullified all his works and authority and power. He brought him to zero.

"Having despoiled the principalities and the powers, he made a show of them openly, triumphing over them in it" (Colossians 2:15). "He stripped principalities and powers naked, making a show of them openly, triumphing over them" (Conybeare). It is a picture of the great Roman general going back to Rome to receive all the plaudits and awards of the senate and of the Caesar. He took behind him all the great nobles and kings who had been in the armies fighting him. They were stripped naked and chained to his chariot. This is the picture that the Holy Spirit uses of the Lord Jesus. He has taken all these powers of darkness, all these satanic forces and chained them, stripped naked, to His triumphal chariot. He has triumphed over them.

The apostle Paul said that he counted everything but loss that he might know Him and the power of His resurrection and the fellowship of His sufferings, being made conformable unto His death. Many believers who have a little understanding of deeper things would put the whole thing another way. They would say, "That I may know Him, being made conformable to His death and the fellowship of His sufferings and the power of His resurrection." They would say that death comes before resurrection. But the apostle Paul put it this way: "That I may know Him and the power of His resurrection." It is because you can never know the death of Christ apart from the resurrection of the Lord Jesus; otherwise, it becomes religion. It is just a question of being dark and heavy and dressing in black and looking miserable—what we call holiness in Christian circles. What a lot of it there is! It is knowing the Lord; it is being alive. To know the Lord, you must have the Holy Spirit; you must know the power of the resurrection of the Lord Jesus and that will lead you to an experience of being conformed to His death and into the fellowship of His sufferings. Woe betide any believer who knows anything about the fellowship of the sufferings of the Lord Jesus without knowing the power of His resurrection. First, you must know the power of His resurrection, or the fellowship of His sufferings will crush you. Now we begin to understand what the apostle Paul had seen, what he had got hold of. He said, "I count everything but loss—my pedigree, my background, my knowledge, my past knowledge—all these things I count but refuse that I may gain Christ, that I may know Him and the power of His resurrection."

"What the exceeding greatness of his power to us-ward who believe." We could talk about the exceeding greatness of His power and leave it at that. We could say all power belongs to God—but it is to us-ward who believe. In other words, the Lord wants you and me to enter into a genuine and living experience of the exceeding greatness of His power. Nothing else will take us through the last phase of world history—no amount of knowledge; no amount of zeal; no amount, even, of fellowship. If we do not have an experience of the exceeding greatness of His power to us-ward, we will never come through. Satan will see to that.

When Paul wrote this letter, there were no chapters and verses. These chapters and verses were put together for us by a monk who went crazy as a result of his endeavours, but we thank God for it because it helps us to move around the Scriptures. But sometimes it is disturbing to the train of thought because we carve things up, as if God has departmentalized things in chapters and verses when in actual fact it is all part of the same thing. "And you did he make alive" (Ephesians 2:1a). Did you get that? "And what the exceeding greatness of his power to us-ward who believe, according to that working of the strength of his might which he wrought in Christ, when he raised him from the dead...and you did he make alive, when ye were dead through your trespasses and sins." Then it says that He made us alive together with Christ and made us to sit together with Christ in heavenly places (see Ephesians 2:5–6). That is absolutely amazing! So this tremendous power is that you and I might know what it is to be made alive together with Christ and raised up together with Him and made to sit together with Him in heavenly places. That takes exceedingly great power. Don't you think this is something that you and I need?

Christ is in the Vessel

"Now unto him that is able to do (that is, has power to do) exceeding abundantly above all that we ask or [even] think" (Ephesians 3:20). It is one thing to ask for something, but some of us are so timid we would not dare to ask but merely think it. "Wouldn't it be lovely if such and such could happen, if the Lord could do this and this in my life?" We dare not actually verbalize it, so we trap it within; but it is there. "Now unto him [who] is able (that is, has power), to do exceeding abundantly above all that we ask or think, according to the power that worketh in us." Now if that power is trapped, if that power in us is ignored, if the law of the Spirit of life in Christ Jesus is not obeyed, not recognized, then God is unable to do exceeding abundantly above all that we ask or think. The power within us is contradicted, is frustrated, is inhibited, is proscribed. In other words, all God's purpose for you and me can be gloriously realized because of the exceeding greatness of His power to us-ward, because by His grace, He has placed within us that power.

In Ephesians 3:16–17a, Paul was praying again: "That he would grant you, according to the riches of his glory, that ye may be strengthened [empowered] with power through his Spirit in the inward man; that Christ may dwell in your hearts through faith." It is the exceeding greatness of His power to us-ward who believe. Do you realize that trapped within that funny little vessel of clay that you call your body is the risen Lord Jesus? Do you realize that Christ is in you, the hope of glory? But we disobey the rules. We ignore Him; we override Him; we contradict Him; we frustrate God's purpose concerning Him in us, and then we end up with no power in us. It is there but it is paralyzed.

"Strengthened or empowered with power through his Spirit in the inward man, that Christ may dwell in your hearts through faith." It is the living Christ manifesting Himself in my mortal body, the living Christ coming through me.

"That ye, being rooted and grounded in love, may be strong to apprehend with all the saints what is the breadth and length and height and depth, and to know the love of Christ which passeth knowledge, that ye may be filled unto all the fulness of God." Ephesians 3:17b–19

Is this a fairy tale? Is it just Christian theology? Is it something that we could just put up in old-fashioned lettering as a little motto on the wall, like they used to in Victorian days? Or is it a living experience? It would be marvellous enough if all we had was Christ dwelling in us through faith, but we are to be rooted and grounded in love to the end that we might be strong to apprehend with all the saints what is the breadth and the length and the height and the depth, to be lost in the infinity of the Lord Jesus, to be lost in the greatness of God, to know the love of Christ which passes knowledge. We are to experience it, not just know about it. We are to know it in experience, to be filled unto all the fulness of God. It would be blasphemy if it was not in the word. How can anyone be filled unto all the fulness of God? All it means is this: Your little capacity is filled to overflowing. Where does it begin? It begins with being empowered with power through His Spirit in the inward man. There is no other way. "Now unto him that is able to do exceeding abundantly above all that we ask or think, according to the power that worketh in us." Then comes the doxology, and so it should.

Whole Power of God is Available to Us

This is the word of God. The trouble with Christians is that they are familiar with the word of God; they think, "I have heard it before." We even sing wonderful hymns about these kinds of things. But oh, how we need the Spirit of wisdom and revelation in the knowledge of the Lord Jesus that the eyes of our hearts might be enlightened to know the exceeding greatness of His power to us-ward who believe. I know that only the Holy Spirit can place it in our heart, but He is well able to do it. It is not a question that we are stupid, but we all are so dim in seeing and dull of hearing. In some ways, we are so familiar with these things that they do not come home to us with all the living power and definition of the Holy Spirit. But if I can say something that the Holy Spirit can put into your heart so that it can roll around in your spirit until, finally, it is illuminated, that will change the whole course and character of your life as a believer and, indeed, our lives as fellowships of believers; and this is it: The whole power of God has been made available to us. Isn't that simple! God, who through a word, created the heavens and the earth; God who spoke the word and there was light; God, who by His word spoke again and again and again and it was done, has made His whole power available to you.

Let me put it another way: He has placed the exceeding greatness of His power at your disposal. Is that going beyond Scripture? Is it going outside of what God has said? I do not think so. This power of God in the early church turned the whole world upside down. They had everything against them—a whole occupying Roman Empire; a whole religious establishment of those who should have seen but did not see; all the security forces; all the powers of government, apart from the invisible forces, powers of darkness and evil; everything was against them. They did not have great missionary training centres or huge theological seminaries and Bible schools. They did not have all the paraphernalia that believers seem to think is absolutely necessary to have to make an impact on this world today. All they had was the Lord Jesus. They had the exceeding greatness of His power, and they turned the world upside down. Jesus Christ is the same yesterday, today, and forever.

Saved to the Uttermost

"Wherefore also he is able [has power] to save to the uttermost them that draw near unto God through him, seeing he ever liveth to make intercession for them." Hebrews 7:25

Did you notice the word uttermost? Let that word uttermost sink into you. He does not just save you barely; He saves you to the uttermost. However depraved your background, whatever the problems are in your family, in your genetic history, whatever you have inherited, whatever cultural problems you have from your background, He is able to save you to the uttermost. He gives you a life, the power of His resurrection, and that life will not rest until it has you home. This resurrection life of the Lord Jesus that is in you and me came from heaven; and through the cross and the resurrection and by the Holy Spirit, it is made available to you and me. It came from heaven; that is its origin, and it will not rest until it has you and me there by His grace.

In Israel, we have one billion birds fly through twice a year. It is the busiest bird traffic lanes in the world. They come from South Africa and East Africa and they go all the way through our narrow little land up to Russia, to Scandinavian, to Eastern Europe. There are great big birds, like the pelicans, so heavy that you wonder how in the world they fly thousands of miles. There are storks that sometimes number as many as thirty thousand, spiraling up into the air so that they are like little specks. You think they are swallows but they are storks with a wing span of three or four feet. Then there are little tiny birds that you think you could blow off course with a breath. These birds are amazing. Who tells them? They do not have a bird automobile association. They do not have bird tracking stations, bird radar, bird electronic services. They do not have anything like that. They have a kind of life in them that will not rest until it brings them right back to where they were born. They do not go by maps or charts, but they have a life inside of them that will not rest. They will fly over thousands and thousands of miles until they come right back to the very spot where they were born.

How much more wonderful it is to have the life of Christ. That eternal life of the Lord Jesus came from heaven, came from God, and will not rest until it gets us back into His presence with exceeding joy. Why should you be so afraid of your circumstances, so afraid of the unknown in your life, always fearful? Everything seems to stick to some Christians. You only have to talk about tribulation and it sticks to them: "Oh dear, I will never do it; I will never do it!" What is wrong with you? Do you think that the Lord Jesus saved you to let you fall by the way? Do you think that He has not provided for you? He came into this world and became Man and died in your place. Is He just going to leave you to the forces of darkness? Is He just going to manipulate you and play with you like a little plaything and then finally destroy you? My dear friend, wake up! God loved you so much that He saved you; He has given you a life and within it there is a power that will not rest until you are back in the presence of God, at the throne of God. Oh, the exceeding greatness of His power!

There are some people who are frightened of death, which is very strange. Long before they die, they are frightened to death. They have only got to see someone else dying and they think they are dying. That is so strange. They hope the Lord does not do that to them, that they will not have to go like that. Why do you cross all those bridges before you come to them? Why don't you take the grace that God has given you for your life? As Sir Charles Haddon Spurgeon once said to a lady who was berating him on this matter: "Madame, you will never have dying grace until you die." You cannot get it and store it in a spiritual deep freeze and bring it out when you need it. God gives you grace to live, grace to overcome, grace for your problems, grace to go through. "Wherefore He is able to save to the uttermost." Do you think that you are an exception? Do you think: "This is for the rest here but not for me"? He will save you to the uttermost. That is the exceeding greatness of His power to you-ward who believe.

God's Power Will Deliver Us from Evil

This exceeding greatness of His power will deliver us from every evil work, every evil spirit. "Who delivered us out of the power of darkness, and [translated] us into the kingdom of the Son of his love" (Colossians 1:13). Oh, the power that took my citizenship out of the kingdom of the power of darkness and transferred me, of all people, into the kingdom of His dear Son! Do you think you did that? The Lord did it for you. He has transferred your citizenship. Satan has no business to play around with you at all. You are redeemed. You do not belong to him. You have been transferred; you have been delivered. God did it. The Lord Jesus took you. Don't let Satan come to you and say that you are his and that he is in charge of these circumstances, that he has a purchase hold on your life. He has no right to you. You have been delivered from the power of darkness, transferred into the kingdom of God's dear Son. You are God's free people. You are not slaves, Egyptian slaves, slaves of some demonic pharaoh. You are free! There are many works of darkness that, one way or another, come into the believer's life. Those works of darkness need to be faced, not in your strength, but in the exceeding greatness of His power. Don't fear; the Lord wants you delivered from every evil work, and He wants you to enjoy all the privileges of being a subject in His kingdom.

Delivered from the Law of Sin and Death

I often think of the very first time I ever travelled on one of the great jumbo jets, and it was in Norway. I had never seen a jumbo jet in my life because they had just come out. As I sat there in my seat, I looked out of the window and it was just the same height as my bedroom window in Britain at the time, which was on the second floor. I could not believe it. There were ten seats across this huge plane with a capacity load of 567, including the crew. It was incredible! I looked all around and thought, "Lord, is this thing ever going to get off the ground?" I watched all the people coming in and wondered if they all had as much luggage as I had. Then I saw all the people coming into the plane, some of them enormous, really huge people, and I thought again, "Oh Lord, is this thing ever going to get off?" I knew that if I got on that runway and ran along it as fast as I possibly could and flapped my arms, I could not get off the ground; and that is only me without luggage. If I got into a car and sped along the runway, I still could not take off. I would just have an accident at the end of the runway.

The one law I have always understood is the law of gravity. I know that if you step off a roof or out of a window you will fall; it is the law of gravity. That great airplane, filled to capacity, cruised down to the end of that runway, very slowly, I thought. Suddenly, that huge thing began to lift, not with tremendous speed, but slowly it began to rise and rise and rise; and within a few moments, we had gone through the clouds into the sunshine. A superior law had overcome the law of gravity.

This is what it says in Romans 8:2: "For the law of the Spirit of life in Christ Jesus made me free from the law of sin and of death." There is something in our lives that is always pulling us down; something in our lives that, somehow, wakes us to works of darkness; something that is like a bias, a tendency always downwards. But the law of the Spirit of life in Christ Jesus, the exceeding greatness of His power to us-ward who believe frees us from this law of sin and death.

Have you ever tried to deal with the law of sin and death? It is like an eider down (as they call it in England), one of those great feather things. You push it here and it comes out there; you push it there and it comes out here. It does not matter where you push it, it will come up somewhere. Many Christians are just like that. They push it down and say, "Ah, I have got it down." Then it comes up behind them, and they push it down again. They spend their whole Christian life doing this, and it is exhausting. No wonder Christians above all people are the most miserable. How exhausting it is to be a Christian when you spend your whole time suppressing things, trying somehow to deal with the law of sin and death. That is not the way. God's way is the Spirit of life in Christ Jesus; and the principle of the Spirit of life in Christ Jesus frees us from sin, and we soar into the heavens. Then we are able to do what we naturally cannot do. Then the impossible becomes possible. Then we live a resurrection life on the other side of the grave, beyond our natural possibilities or talents or energies.

God's Power Is Able to Keep Us

"Unto an inheritance incorruptible, and undefiled, and that fadeth not away, reserved in heaven for you, who by the power of God are [kept] through faith unto a salvation ready to be revealed in the last time." I Peter 1:4–5

Did you hear that? God does not just save us; He keeps us. How does He keep us? We are kept by the power of God.

Why are Christians afraid of the power of God? Why are we afraid, sometimes, of the power of the Holy Spirit? He is the only means by which God can keep us unto an inheritance incorruptible, undefiled, uncompromised, which does not fade away. Are you going to lose your inheritance, so dearly won for you? You do not have to. You can be kept by the power of God. All the way through the circumstances of your life, through its ups and downs, through its sunshine and through its storms, through its light and through its shadows, you can be kept by the power of God. What a testimony! What a testimony, finally, to be able to say, "Thine is the power forever. It is Your exceeding great power that has saved me to the uttermost. It is Your exceeding great power that has delivered me from the powers of darkness and transferred me into the kingdom of Your dear Son. It is Your exceeding great power that has guarded me unto this inheritance incorruptible." Dear child of God, wake up! God has made this power available to you. He has placed it at your disposal.

Overcoming Power

This exceeding greatness of His power is able to overcome in you, whatever your problems. Everybody has a special problem. It is very strange how everyone has their own special problems; and when they come to talk to you, they are always the most difficult, apparently. The Scots tell me they are very difficult; the Irish tell me they are very difficult; the Dutch tell me they are very obstinate and difficult; the Germans tell me they are very difficult, along with the Japanese and the Chinese. They all have a reason, and it is something quite unique with each one that, in their mind, makes it very difficult for them to go on with the Lord; they cannot overcome. But you have the exceeding greatness of His power that is able to overcome whatever your racial inheritance, whatever your cultural inheritance, whatever your social inheritance, whatever your physical inheritance from your family is. Whatever the defects in your personality or temperament, you have a life within you which is able to overcome.

I know of no better illustration than the one I have used for many, many years. When you go to the mountains, no matter where these mountains might be, you will often see a great magnificent tree and at its foot there will be a great boulder split in two. It would have been easy to imagine that tree, when it was full grown, suddenly fell on this boulder and split the thing in two. No! Do you know how that great tree began? It began as a little bit of what looked like dried-up wood the size of my small fingernail. That little tiny piece of dried-up wood, a seed, fell into a fissure in that boulder. You could have said to it: "You silly little thing.

What do you think you are doing? You have fallen into this fissure. Do you think you are going to overcome this great boulder? Do you know how many tons this great boulder weighs? Do you know how strong it is? Do you realize what equipment it would take to break this boulder open and how many men it would take to do it? You silly little thing."

But if that little seed could talk, it would say, "I have a life within me, and the life within me will overcome."

A little later when you go back and look at this funny little seed, two or three little white things that look like hairs have gone down and you think, "How stupid! I have never seen anything weaker than those funny little white hairs. What are you doing?"

"These are my roots."

"Roots!"

"What do you think you are going to do with those little roots?"

"I am overcoming."

"Overcoming? You are overcoming this boulder?"

"Yes, I am overcoming this boulder."

"You stupid little thing!"

Later, when you go back, another little white shoot, about an inch, has gone up, a little more green than the ones that went down. And you say, "What is that?"

"That is going to be my trunk."

"Your trunk!"

"Yes, my trunk."

"You stupid thing! Do you realize that you have a great boulder all around you? There is no way you are going to overcome."

"Oh yes," the seed says, "I have a life within me, and this life will overcome."

If that little seed obeys the law of the life within it, it will overcome. It will grow; its roots will go down; it will feed somewhere, in some kind of moisture, in some kind of soil, however scarce, within that boulder. Its shoots will go up into the sunlight and into the air, and lo and behold, when you come back a few years later, there will be the huge boulder split and a great tree has grown out of the boulder. What was impossible has happened.

If you have a life within you—that is, the life of the Lord Jesus, the power of His resurrection—nothing is impossible. It will break open all the great boulders of your circumstances; all the boulders of your situations and difficulties; all the things that you think will destroy you and are impossible, that are so complex and so difficult. Obey the law of the Spirit of life in Christ Jesus, and that boulder will be broken.

I can give you another illustration. Have you ever watched salmon? They are amazing creatures. Many times in Norway I have watched salmon leaping up in those rivers and falling back, up and falling back, up and falling back, then up and over and they swim a little. I feel so sorry for them when those fishermen get them. It swims for a little, going higher; and then it comes to a rapid and it jumps and jumps and jumps; then it goes over. It is amazing. I understand they come all the way from the Caribbean and they go up the very river they came from. The difficulties that they meet are enormous, but they will not rest until they get back to the very pool from which they came. Isn't it extraordinary!

We could say to the salmon: "Look here, you are making your life very difficult. You do not need to do all this. Why don't you take an easier way; stay in the pool here."

"No, there is something in me; I have got to go on."

It is an overcoming life. It is salmon life, and it will overcome every difficulty that faces the salmon until it gets back to where it came from. You have something far more than salmon life; you have eternal life. You have the resurrection life of the Lord Jesus, the exceeding greatness of His power to us-ward who believe.

God's Power Will Transform You

The exceeding greatness of His power will transform you. I do not know who you are; but you cannot have gone very far with the Lord before you begin to despair that you will ever be like Him. The more you go on with the Lord, the more, sometimes, you despair that you will ever be like Him. But the exceeding greatness of His power will transform you. It is a life that can do no other than transform you. In II Corinthians 3:18, it tells us that as we behold His glory as in a mirror, we will be changed into the same likeness. We shall be changed by His Spirit into the same likeness.

There is an illustration that brings this home. Have you ever watched a butterfly emerge from a chrysalis? Isn't it amazing the contortions it goes through? To the eye that is uneducated in this kind of thing, the chrysalis is very ugly but the butterfly is very beautiful. How is it that out of something so uninteresting, so dull, almost ugly, something so beautiful can come? It has butterfly life; it is as simple as that. It has the life of a butterfly; it can do no other. It will go into a chrysalis, and then at the right time, through enormous contortions and seeming agonies, it will emerge in another dimension.

If you have the life of Christ in you, if you have the exceeding greatness of His power in you, you may seem to be a very ugly chrysalis; but somewhere within that chrysalis is all the beauty of the Lord Jesus. You may go through contortions, through agonies, through tribulations, but in the end, you will be transformed into His likeness. It is the life that is in you.

The only thing we can say is, "Thine is the power. It came from You; it will end with You."

There is another point: Who believe. "And what the exceeding greatness of His power to us-ward who believe." That is the problem. It does not mean to just believe doctrine; it means you actually have living faith.

The Church Is the Vehicle of God's Power

The last point I want to make is that Christ's body, the church should be and is meant to be, is built to be the manifestation of the exceeding greatness of His power. It is very interesting that in Ephesians, after having talked about us knowing personally the exceeding greatness of his power, Paul goes on to say, "He put all things in subjection under his feet, and gave him to be head over all things to the church, which is his body, the fulness of him that filleth all in all" (Ephesians 1:22–23).

In Acts 1:1 it says, "The former treatise I made, O Theophilus, concerning all that Jesus began both to do and to teach." So Luke's gospel is the beginning of what Jesus began to teach and to do, and Acts is the continuation; only this time, it is through the body. The Head is at the right hand of God, and now it is through the body. The church is created to be the vessel of His power—Head and body together. When the church relegates the power to itself, it backslides. It becomes like some cancerous growth. But the church is meant to be the expression of the power that belongs to God. That does not mean the church does not have the power; it is to be the vehicle of that power, to be the vessel of that power, to be the instrument of that power. That is why the apostle

Paul, speaking of himself, said, "I came amongst you in fear and trembling, not in words of wisdom but in demonstration of the Spirit and of power." What a tremendous need there is for us to know not only the truth but the power of God. In our fellowships, we need to know the Lord with us in power—power to change, power to deliver, power to save, power to heal. We know that some of this has been taken to extreme, but that does not in any way negate the truth.

The kingdom of God is not in word but in power. When the kingdom of God is not in power, you do not really have a functioning church. The church may be there potentially, but it is not functioning. When the power of God is present, the body makes increase, building itself up, so that every part functions as it ought to. How we need to know this exceeding greatness of His power!

Why are so many young people going to all kinds of occult things? Why are they going off to all the eastern religions? In some strange way, they find within these things something that works. It is evil, but there is something that works in these things. Sometimes, we have reduced the church to a matter of theology and truth but have not realized that it is meant to be the power of God visiting our community and locality. Look at the early church and see what happened. Or, look at the beginning of every great move of the Holy Spirit in the history of the church and you will find the exceeding greatness of His power displayed in men and women torn out of their depraved condition and brought into living union with the Lord Jesus. They became human beings able to love, able to live, able to lay down their lives.

Everywhere you look in the history of the church, in the beginning of every one of the great movements of the Holy Spirit, you will see the same thing. The Quakers turned Britain upside down at one point. Two-thirds of their ministering brethren were in prison. What did they do? They turned the prisons into Bible schools, and inmate after inmate after inmate got saved and came out of those prisons as servants of God. Think what the early Puritans did. People think of Puritans as legalists, but they were not in their beginnings. They turned society in Britain upside down with the power of God that was in them. Think of the early Evangelical Awakening, that we now call the Methodists, and what they did in transforming the social conditions in Britain. It was not by a social gospel but by the power of the living Christ that they saved Britain from the French Revolution. Wherever you turn, you see the power of God.

This is what we need in the last days of church history as we move into the last phase of things. We need the power of God, the exceeding greatness of His power. There may come a time when we shall not be able to meet. There may be a time when we can only gather with five or six in homes or out in forests or caves, but the exceeding greatness of His power is the same. It does not have to be in some comfortable auditorium, but that power of His can be manifested anywhere, at any time, in any circumstance, in any condition. May God give us the grace that we may know the exceeding greatness of His power to us-ward as the church. What is the point of talking about the church—its nature, its character, its destiny—if we are not experiencing the exceeding greatness of His power? May the Lord help us, may He visit us, may He open our eyes, and may our experience be His exceeding great power.

Then I think we shall have only one response now or when we face the Lord: "Thine is the power for ever. Amen." It did not begin with us; it did not have its source in us. It was His power that came to us, that saved us, kept us, delivered us, transformed us, overcame within us, and enabled us to be an expression of the body of the Lord Jesus in our day and generation.

May the Lord do this in us.

3.
Experiencing the Exceeding Greatness of His Power

Ephesians 1:15–23

For this cause I also, having heard of the faith in the Lord Jesus which is among you, and the love which ye show toward all the saints, cease not to give thanks for you, making mention of you in my prayers; that the God of our Lord Jesus Christ, the Father of glory, may give unto you a spirit of wisdom and revelation in the knowledge of him; having the eyes of your heart enlightened, that ye may know what is the hope of his calling, what the riches of the glory of his inheritance in the saints, and what the exceeding greatness of his power to us-ward who believe, according to that working of the strength of his might which he wrought in Christ, when he raised him from the dead, and made him to sit at his right hand in the heavenly places, far above all rule, and authority, and power, and dominion, and every name that is named, not only in this world, but also in that which is to come: and he put all things in subjection under his feet, and gave him to be head over all things to the church, which is his body, the fulness of him that filleth all in all.

Ephesians 3:16,20

That he would grant you, according to the riches of his glory, that ye may be strengthened with power through his Spirit in the inward man ... Now unto him that is able to do exceeding abundantly above all that we ask or think, according to the power that worketh in us.

Acts 1:4–5

And, being assembled together with them, [Jesus] charged them not to depart from Jerusalem,

but to wait for the promise of the Father, which, said he, ye heard from me: for John indeed baptized with water; but ye shall be baptized in the Holy Spirit not many days hence.

Luke 24:48–49

Ye are witnesses of these things. And behold, I send forth the promise of my Father upon you: but tarry ye in the city, until ye be clothed with power from on high.

II Corinthians 4:7–12

But we have this treasure in earthen vessels, that the exceeding greatness of the power may be of God, and not from ourselves; we are pressed on every side, yet not straitened; perplexed, yet not unto despair; pursued, yet not forsaken; smitten down, yet not destroyed;

always bearing about in the body the dying of Jesus, that the life also of Jesus may be manifested in our body. For we who live are always delivered unto death for Jesus' sake, that the life also of Jesus may be manifested in our mortal flesh. So then death worketh in us, but life in you.

If the power belongs to God and the exceeding greatness of that power is made available to us-ward who believe, should we not take it to the full? Should we not live in it to the full extent of what God, through the Lord Jesus, has so dearly won for us?

How can we experience the exceeding greatness of His power? We know that it is to us-ward. In other words, it is for us; it has been made available to us. The Lord Jesus, in His work on the cross, has won for us this exceeding greatness of divine power. It is made available to us; it is at our disposal. It is not that you and I are special people, elite people, that we have qualities that qualify us for such power. It is simply that the Lord Jesus died for sinners that we might know the exceeding greatness of God's power to bring us from where we are now to where He wants us to be. Nothing other than the exceeding greatness of His power can do that. No amount of intelligence, no amount of zeal, no amount of knowledge—biblical or otherwise—no amount of devotion, even, will ever get us there. It requires the exceeding greatness of God's power to get us to the place where God wants us to be; to bring us to the place where we are transformed, changed into the likeness of the Lord Jesus; to bring us to the place where we can reign with Him; to bring us to the place where we can be the bride of the Lord Jesus, the wife of the Lamb. There is nothing other than the exceeding greatness of God's power that can do that. It is not given to special people, elite people, superior people; it is given to any sinner who has been saved by the grace of God.

All the power of the Godhead is made available to a sinner saved by the grace of God. Once that sinks into us, we have to wonder why we do not experience this power; why the general level of experience is one of inhibition, one of inability. We know we are unable, we know we are weak, we know that in ourselves we cannot reach God's end; but since God has made available to us the exceeding greatness of His power, why do we not experience the exceeding greatness of this power? It is a good question. What is it that holds us back in this whole matter? How can you and I genuinely, progressively experience the power of His resurrection? Is it possible? I say it is possible only by the Spirit of God and by the work of the cross. The Holy Spirit can never fully, powerfully express Himself progressively in a human life without the work of the cross. But the work of the cross needs all the exceeding greatness of God's power for it to be efficient, for it to be operative and effective in a human life. Otherwise, it becomes dead, heavy religion.

The Work of the Holy Spirit

There is absolutely no way to experience the resurrection life of the Lord Jesus except by the Holy Spirit. Until Pentecost, until Shavuot, until the time when the Holy Spirit was poured out, those 120 faithful believers in the upper room, who were absolutely one, could only see the work of the cross and the resurrection of the Lord Jesus as an objective, historical fact. In other words, they knew He was risen from the dead, they knew that He was alive, they knew that He was the Messiah, they knew that God had raised Him from the dead, they even knew that He had ascended because they had been witnesses of His ascension, and they knew that He was coming back, but the whole thing was objective. It was a kind of objective, historical fact. They knew that He was alive from the dead, but that resurrection life was not in them. It was merely something they believed with all their heart. They were witnesses of it, but that resurrection life and power was not in them. It was not a subjective experience of theirs; it could only be an objective, historical fact.

The tragedy is that for millions of Christian believers, the resurrection of Jesus is still merely a historical fact. They know nothing about the power of His resurrection in their life; they know nothing about the exceeding greatness of His power. But when the Holy Spirit came on that day of Pentecost, on that Shavuot, something happened when Jesus received the promise of the Father and poured out the Holy Spirit.

Some people think that the significance of Pentecost was gifts—that they prophesied, they spoke in tongues—and that there was wind and fire. Now I believe firmly in such gifts, and I believe that they are still operative today. I am not afraid of wind and fire—the more of it, the better. But the fact of the matter is, they are the outward things. What happened on Pentecost was that the life and power of the risen Lord Jesus became available to 120 poor, saved sinners. Into those 120 believers, who, before, could only know Jesus objectively, suddenly came the risen power and life of the Lord Jesus. Those 120 units in a congregation suddenly became 120 members sharing a body. From that moment, those believers could begin to experience what the apostle Paul said in Ephesians 3:16–19: "That he would grant you, according to the riches of his glory, that ye may be strengthened with power through his Spirit in the inward man; that Christ may dwell in your hearts [in you] through faith; to the end that ye, being rooted and grounded in love, may be strong to apprehend with all the saints what is the breadth and length and height and depth, and to know the love of Christ which passeth knowledge, that ye may be filled unto all the fulness of God."

It became their experience, weak as they were, poor as they were. We know only a few of the names of those believers; they were so insignificant. But those 120 became the recipients of something so tremendous that it was the fulfilment of all the burden of the prophets. It was the promise of the Father. Would to God we all had such an experience of the Lord Jesus through the Holy Spirit.

"Now unto him that is able to do exceeding abundantly above all that we ask or think, according to the power that worketh in us" (Ephesians 3:20). For the first time, the power was in them. Something had come from without to within. Something had moved from one dimension to another. Is it any wonder that the world was turned upside down? Is it any wonder that in spite of all the might of Rome and all the opposition and antagonism of the religious establishment, in spite of all the problems of weakness, failings, sin and transgression amongst themselves, the whole known world was turned up-side down and inside out? Something happened! It was the exceeding greatness of God's power. It was the power of the resurrection of the Lord Jesus.

The Baptism of the Holy Spirit

In Acts 1, we are told that the Lord Jesus, having taught them all things concerning the kingdom of God, told them that they were not to depart from Jerusalem but to wait for the promise of the Father, which they heard from Him. Then He explains it:

"For John indeed baptized with water; but ye shall be baptized in the Holy Spirit not many days hence." Acts 1:5

I realize the moment that we start to talk about the baptism of the Spirit, all kinds of prejudice, bigotry, resistance comes in. You can almost see it with some folks. They become almost nervous: "Oh, don't talk about the baptism of the Spirit; it is very, very dangerous. We do not want people falling all over the place, weird things happening, excessive emotion, and strange things. We have had enough of it." It is amazing the prejudices that this term baptism of the Spirit arouses in believers. In the same way, the word Israel arouses the same kind of antagonism in many believers. It is strange. Years ago, it used to be true of the cross, as well. Once you started talking about the working of the cross, prejudice rose up. It is almost as if the flesh cannot bear anything like this.

Now I am not saying that everything that is taught concerning the baptism of the Spirit is right, but I want you to see that the term is very much in the word of God; and we need to face it.

In Matthew 3:11, John the Baptist said, "I indeed baptize you in water unto repentance: but he that cometh after me is mightier than I, whose shoes I am not worthy to bear: he shall baptize you in the Holy Spirit and in fire: whose fan is in his hand, and he will thoroughly cleanse his threshing-floor; and he will gather his wheat into the garner, but the chaff he will burn up with unquenchable fire." This is recorded in all three synoptic gospels; that is how important it is. It is in Mark 1:7–8, Luke 3:16–17; and then we find it again in the words of the Lord Jesus Himself in Acts 1:4–5.

I think it is very interesting that John the Baptist described the heart of his ministry, the character of his ministry as baptizing in water. In other words, he did not go into a whole long spiel about what he was called to, about what he was trying to do, about his great preaching of repentance; he said the heart of his ministry was baptizing in water. That was the heart and character of it. It was a baptism expressing repentance, turning away from sin, and getting prepared for the coming of the Messiah. But he described the heart and character of the work of the Lord Jesus as: "He will baptize in the Spirit and with fire." Now I find this very extraordinary. If this matter is peripheral, if this matter is optional, if it is something on the surface, why did John the Baptist—the greatest of all the prophets, according to the Lord Jesus Himself—describe the heart and character of the ministry of the Lord Jesus as being: "He shall baptize in the Spirit and in fire"?

The Work of the Holy Spirit Is Vital

Another thing about this extraordinary statement is that the work of the Lord Jesus is vital, essential, central, and strategic. The heart and character of the ministry of the Lord Jesus is what He did on the cross; but as far as He was concerned, it was what He was winning for us on the cross. That is the vital thing. It is not just a forgiveness of sins, not just a cancellation of sins, not just a justification in the sight of God, but it is the possibility of being joined to God by the Spirit of the Lord in Christ. It is therefore vital. The word vital means "living." In other words, you can have no life apart from this. You can know what it is that Jesus did on the cross, you can know that He died to forgive sins, you can know that He would convert and save; but apart from the Holy Spirit, there is nothing living. He is the One who makes it vital. It is vital.

The Work of the Holy Spirit Is Central, Essential, and Strategic

The second thing is that it is central. In other words, there is nothing in the whole work of God, in the kingdom of God, in the purpose of God that can be done apart from the Holy Spirit. It is absolutely central to everything that God would do. Therefore, it is essential; it is not something that is optional. Some people think: "I am interested in all this, but this is Pentecostalism, isn't it?" No, my dear friends; get that clear out of your heads. It is like saying that baptism by immersion is something to do with Baptists. That is absolute nonsense. What does the word of God say? There can be absolutely nothing as far as knowing the kingdom of God, knowing the purpose of God in reality, knowing the body of Christ effectively functioning apart from the Holy Spirit. His Person and work is central to it. In God's whole plan, in His whole strategy, this is vital to it; it is strategic. Wherever we look in the history of the church, we find that in every great move of the Spirit, God has taken men and women and brought them into a living experience of the exceeding greatness of His power. It has turned human society upside down all over the world.

Baptism Is by Immersion

John the Baptist spoke of the Lord Jesus as the One who would baptize in the Holy Spirit and in fire. My understanding of baptism is that it is by immersion, not sprinkling. I find it very interesting that years ago there was a kind of conspiracy amongst a whole number of orthodox, institutional denominations to keep certain truths buried. For instance, in Israel, when they discovered the Qumran and the Dead Sea Caves and the scrolls that were in them, they found certain baptisteries all over the community. Since then, in our excavations in Jerusalem and elsewhere, we have found that there were baptisteries everywhere. They had always tried to tell us that there was no such thing as baptism in Jewish circles, that it was something quite new with John the Baptist. Then they began to say that these were cisterns, not baptisteries, and that is why there were so many of them. But in the War of 1967, when the Jewish authorities finally came into possession of the Qumran, they made their investigations and said these were not cisterns; they were baptisteries. We suddenly discovered that baptism was not by sprinkling; it was by immersion. This was a terrible shock to the institutional denominations. They have been strangely quiet about the whole subject ever since.

God does not sprinkle you with the Holy Spirit. He does not make a little mark on your head, surface deep, with a little bit of the Holy Spirit. He puts you right under. He immerses you into the Holy Spirit; He buries you in the Holy Spirit; He envelopes you in the Holy Spirit. That is the work of the Lord Jesus. The

Holy Spirit had touched people before under the Old Covenant; He had even come upon people in the Old Covenant; He even spoke from within them in the Old Covenant. But this was the great mark of the New Covenant: The Lord Jesus would take sinners, saved by His grace and justified by His work on the cross, and immerse them in the Holy Spirit and in fire.

Jesus Is the Baptizer

Then I want you to notice one other thing about this extraordinary statement which is so often overlooked: It is Jesus who is the Baptizer. The word of God does not say so much about the baptism of the Spirit; it speaks about Jesus as the Baptizer in the Holy Spirit, putting the whole emphasis on the fact that He, through His finished work, is the One who takes you and puts the Holy Spirit in you and immerses you into the Holy Spirit.

God Provides Nothing Outside of Christ

What does all this mean? Let me make a few statements that I hope will help. First, God provides nothing outside of Christ. The Lord Jesus is the Alpha and the Omega; the beginning and the end; the first and the last of everything of God, everything that is to do with God. God gives us everything in Christ. There is nothing outside of Him; everything is in Him.

We Cannot Experience Christ
Apart from the Holy Spirit

The second thing is that we can know, we can experience nothing of Christ and nothing of that which is given us in Christ apart from the Holy Spirit. You cannot know or experience anything that God has given you in Christ, you cannot even experience the Lord Jesus Himself apart from the Holy Spirit. Without the Holy Spirit, it is religion, Christianized religion, of which there is an enormous amount in Christian circles, including evangelical circles and, may I dare to say, even in charismatic circles. It is man's psychology, man's power, man's energy, man's talents, man's ways, the system of this world, the fashion of this world— all in the guise of the Lord Jesus. Apart from the Holy Spirit, we can know nothing.

Neither repentance, nor conviction of sin, nor living faith, nor spiritual birth, nor spiritual growth, nor spiritual character, nor spiritual training, nor anointing for service, nor transformation into the likeness of Christ can come apart from the Holy Spirit. It means you cannot even repent without the Holy Spirit. You cannot know conviction of sin apart from the Holy Spirit. You cannot ever know the gift of living faith apart from the Holy Spirit. You can never be born of God apart from the Holy Spirit. You can never grow in the Lord apart from the Holy Spirit. You can never be trained and corrected apart from the Holy Spirit. You can never discover the Lord Jesus apart from the Holy Spirit. You can never be changed into the likeness of Christ apart from the Holy Spirit. There can be no anointing apart from the Holy Spirit.

There is an error in Christian circles that is as terrible as any of the heresies that have weakened and destroyed the church. It is that you can have Jesus without the Holy Spirit. Our Lord Jesus is at the right hand of God, from whence He shall return. He is God located, God expressed. When people speak of Jesus as if He is the Holy Spirit, they do a great injustice to Him and to the word of God. Of course, the Lord Jesus is God the Son; therefore, He is everywhere, He is infinite. But the fact of the matter is that you can only know the infinite life of Jesus by the Spirit; you can only experience the infinite power of the resurrection life of Jesus by the Spirit.

Therefore, can you see what Satan has done in this matter to bring such an enormous prejudice concerning the work of the Holy Spirit? We speak of the Father and the Son, but the Spirit is an "it." Why do we do this? It is because the Holy Spirit is always, if I may so use the term, defacing Himself, devaluing Himself. (I hate to put it this way.) He keeps Himself in the background. He never draws attention to Himself. It is always Jesus, the Lord Jesus whom the Holy Spirit is pointing to and unveiling. The things of God in Christ and through Christ are the things that the Holy Spirit reveals to us.

What a wonderful thing it is to know the Holy Spirit. I thank God the day I got to know the Holy Spirit. He can be grieved, and only a person can be grieved. The Holy Spirit, loving, gentle as a dove, is as powerful and strong as a raging fire. It is amazing how gentle the Holy Spirit is with us, sometimes how quiet He is, how tender He is, how understanding He is, how sensitive He is; but make no mistake about it, you can grieve the Holy Spirit and you can quench Him. Then all your knowledge of Jesus becomes religion; then your whole life becomes a facade; then the whole thing is an artificiality. Witness church history.

The Two Works of the Holy Spirit

"Now on the last day, the great day of the feast, Jesus stood and cried, saying, "If any man thirst, let him come unto me and drink. He that believeth on me, as the Scripture hath said, from within him shall flow rivers of living water. But this spake he of the Spirit, which they that believed on him were to receive: for the Spirit was not yet given; because Jesus was not yet glorified". John 7:37–39

I am sure that on this matter we all are absolutely one —that the Holy Spirit was not poured out or given until the day of Pentecost. But then we have the most extraordinary thing in John 20:19–23. It says, "When therefore it was evening, on that day, the first day of the week, and when the doors were shut where the disciples were, for fear of the Jews, Jesus came and stood in the midst, and saith unto them, Peace be unto you. And when he had said this, he showed unto them his hands and his side. The disciples therefore were glad, when they saw the Lord. Jesus therefore said to them again, Peace be unto you: as the Father hath sent me, even so send I you. And when he had said this, he breathed on them, and saith unto them, Receive ye the Holy Spirit: whose so ever sins ye forgive, they are forgiven unto them; whose so ever sins ye retain, they are retained."

I have heard some extraordinary things about this passage. I have heard people teach that Jesus actually gave them the Holy

Spirit that day. Now we are in a mess. Did He or did He not? If the Lord Jesus gave those disciples the Spirit that day by breathing on them and saying "Receive ye the Holy Spirit," why didn't He do the same with Thomas the next time He appeared to them? Thomas said he did not believe they had seen Him. He said he had to see with his own eyes and put his hands in those nail prints in His hands and in His side before he would believe. Eight days later, Jesus came again to His disciples and Thomas was with them. Now you probably would have said: "Thomas, come here and put your hand in these nail prints"; and he would have done it. Then Thomas would have said: "My Lord and my God." Then you would have said: "Now Thomas, you have missed something vital. The Lord is going to breathe on you and say, 'Receive ye the Holy Spirit.'"

What was the Lord Jesus doing unless He was seeking to make clear, to define something that would happen on the day of Pentecost concerning two things that were going to happen together? The Holy Spirit was going to come to indwell and empower. It was almost as if the Lord Jesus said not to mix up the two things. They can be together; but generally speaking, they are not. I want you to know that there is something quiet about this. "Receive ye the Holy Spirit" is very quiet. The indwelling of the Holy Spirit is something so marvellous; it is the characteristic of the New Covenant. But it can be so quiet that you hardly know He is there. Then think of the day of Pentecost. There came the wind and the whole place shook like an earthquake and tongues of fire came and settled on every one of them. Something very different happened.

The Indwelling of the Holy Spirit

The producing of character may be agonizing, but it is very quiet. The producing of fruit is so quiet. Have you heard fruit making a noise? Some people dig up things all the time to see if they are growing. If you go out every day to inspect the fruit trees, you may see a little tiny bud on a tree and the next day there is a little nodule not bigger than the top of my little finger. When you go out a day or two later, you still can hardly see it, but week after week it grows quietly. There is no great noise about it, no thunderstorms, no great wind or fire. It is all very quiet, but it grows and grows. The fruit of the Spirit—love, joy, peace—is just the same. It grows quietly, progressively, in almost a still manner. You hardly know it is happening, and yet everybody else can see it. "Look what is happening in that life. The beauty of the Lord is there; the character of the Lord is there; there is something beautiful in that person."

When we are born, we cry. That is the first thing that happens. When we are born physically, we are banged and we cry. And so it is when we are born of God. The Holy Spirit comes with no great wind or great fire. When we accept the Lord Jesus, it is very quiet; but we all know someone is born because they let out a yell. I don't mean physically, but we all know; it is very quiet.

Look at a baby. I know that you all have problems with babies sometimes because they keep you up at night; they wail and a lot of other things. When I was young, I wailed so much my mother took me to a specialist. She said to him: "My son cries so much, and I am fed up with all the neighbours coming around and telling me that he is crying. I have done everything. I feed him, I give him dummies, I give him toys, I cuddle him, and still he cries." The specialist said, "He is a crying baby. Unfortunately, madam, you have a very strong-willed son and this is the sign: They cry and cry and cry. Wheel him down to the end of your garden and leave him there." That is exactly what my mother did. We had a huge garden in a great mansion of a house in those days after I was first born. So my mother would put me in the pram and wheel me down to the garden and leave me there. The neighbours would come running to tell my mother that her baby was crying and had been crying for a solid hour. My mother would say, "Let him!"

The Empowering of the Holy Spirit

When we are born of God, we cry. There is something wrong if a person is born of the Spirit and you do not hear a cry, you do not even know there is a movement of life. Of course, we know. But being clothed with power from on high is something very different. We all know when a person is clothed with power from on high. They may not always be so conscience of it, but suddenly, into their ministry, into their life, into their whole contribution comes an authority, a real authority; it is a God-given authority. There comes a divine ability to do things. There comes a divine discernment, a sensitivity to the Lord that was never there before. It is the work of the Holy Spirit. You have this two-fold work—the indwelling of the Holy Spirit and the empowering of the Holy Spirit.

Now the exceeding greatness of His power has much to do with the empowering of His Spirit. Of course, it also has to do with the indwelling.

I think of this wonderful Scripture: "Ye shall be clothed with power from on high." What a beautiful phrase that is. When a person is rightly clothed, you are not self-conscious; you can get on with the job. When you are painting a house, you do not paint it in your best suit. Otherwise, if you are like me, you are going to be worried all the time. It makes you self-conscious, nervous, almost neurotic. So you get dressed in the right thing.

People make such a lot of fuss over this kind of thing. Oftentimes, they will say things like this to me: "Do you believe in the gifts of the Holy Spirit?"

"Yes, I do."

"Do you believe that they are for today?"

"Yes, I do."

Then they say, "Jesus is enough for me. I do not need the gifts; He is enough."

I always say, "Jesus is enough for me as well, but I see it differently from you. I see those gifts as gifts of Jesus. I do not see them as Jesus and gifts; I see the gifts as another gift of Jesus, something more of Jesus expressed, something more of Jesus to be contributed."

Other people say to me: "You know, I do not like all this talk about being clothed with power from on high. Most of the people I know who believe this thing are all big wind bags. They do all kinds of strange things."

All I can say is that there is a lot that is wrong, just like there is an awful lot of marriage ending in divorce; but we do not stop getting married. They say that the greatest number of people who die, die of food poisoning; but we do not stop eating. It is so silly.

When someone says that they want character, they want to grow in the Lord, thank God for that. But if I had to have an operation, I would not want to know that the surgeon who is going to operate upon me has the most marvellous moral character in the United States; that he is an honest man, a loving man, an upright man, a moral man; that he is full of personality and character. I would not even want to know that he has all those degrees after his name. I would want to know if he has the right equipment as well as the right skill. I would not want him coming at me with a tree saw and a mallet. I would want him to have the right equipment to be able to do the job that he has to do. Of course, it is absolutely essential that we should be like the Lord, that we should have the character of the Lord, but we need also to have the power of the Holy Spirit.

I always remind myself that our Lord Jesus was born of the Spirit at Bethlehem. He was indwelt of the Holy Spirit. He was tempted in all points like as we are, yet by the indwelling of the Holy Spirit, He overcame. But when He was thirty years of age, He was anointed with the Holy Spirit. Now if He needed an anointing of the Holy Spirit thirty years later in order to do the work of God and fulfil what God had given Him to do, how much more do I?

To know and experience the exceeding greatness of His power, to know that power working in us, to know the power of His resurrection, we need all the work of the Holy Spirit. The wonderful thing is that the whole work of the Holy Spirit is available to us, and it is the Lord Jesus who introduces us. He is the One who brings the Holy Spirit within us; He is the One who anoints us with the Holy Spirit. May God sink this word into your heart.

The Work of the Cross

The work of the cross is, of course, as important as the work of the Holy Spirit. I do not have to tell you that the great problem in the Christian life, the great problem in our fellowships, the great problem in Christian work is "I." It is the self-life in you and me; we are the problem. Now it is not just the sinful "I," the immoral "I," the adulterous "I," which is bad enough; but it is the clever "I," the intelligent "I," the gifted "I," the ingenious "I"—that is the problem. The work of the Lord and the church of God has suffered more from its gifted members than its ungifted ones.

Let me give you a few examples. There is a man with organizing ability. He gets his hands upon the work of God, and within a matter of a very short time, he has organized the whole thing and organized the Holy Spirit clean out of it. He believes that he is gifted. He is an organizer, but his gift has never gone through Calvary. It has never been let go of at the cross and buried, and it has never been given back in resurrection life. Therefore, the poison of hell is in it. However gifted or clever a person, the church cannot be built with that uncrucified gift. One may have the gift of speech, but it does not necessarily turn a person into a preacher. One may speak wonderfully, eloquently, be a great orator; but unless it has gone to the cross and been let go of, been buried with Christ and given back in the life of Christ, it never gets anywhere.

Thank God for great intellects like the apostle Paul, but what happens when those intellects have never gone to Calvary? They destroy; they do not build up. Think of the great gifts of singing and music and so much else in the church. How we thank God for these gifts! But we all know the difference when we hear one person singing and we hear them, and we hear another person singing and we hear the Lord. One person plays and we are left with their tremendous technique; another person plays and we are in the presence of God. Why is it that the same gift can introduce us into the presence of the Lord in one person and leave us with the person in another? It is because it has never gone through Calvary.

If you want to know the power of His resurrection, you have to know the death of His cross. There is no way to go into the power of His resurrection life without first being identified with Him in His death. In other words, the work of the cross is the regulator of spiritual life. That means the Holy Spirit can come upon you and you can have a tremendous experience of the Holy Spirit; but having begun in the Spirit, you can end in the flesh. It is because when the work of the cross is not known, "I" takes over; and almost imperceptibly, instead of it being the Holy Spirit and the Lord Jesus, it is now me. It is self-life. I begin to use my ministry for my own self-fulfilment. I begin to use my gift to manipulate other people. I begin to use the fellowship of God as a platform for my dictatorship. Unless we know the work of the cross, the Holy Spirit will be grieved and, in the end, quenched. The only safety we have is the work of the cross. I think of those wonderful words: "I have been crucified with Christ; nevertheless

I live, yet not I, but Christ liveth in me: and the life which I now live I live by the faith of the Son of God, who loved me and gave himself for me" (see Galatians 2:20). There is an "I" life. "I" has been crucified; "I" has been crossed out. Something tremendous has happened to "I." The self has gone through Calvary and is now a vehicle for God.

"But we have this treasure in earthen vessels (pots of clay, vessels of clay), that the exceeding greatness of the power may be of God, and not from ourselves; pressed on every side, yet not straitened; perplexed, yet not unto despair; pursued, yet not forsaken; smitten down, yet not destroyed" (II Corinthians 4:7–9). Pressed, perplexed, pursued, smitten down. This does not sound like a normal catalogue in a Christian testimony, does it? One would feel that this man needs to go to a deliverance ministry. He needs to get absolutely delivered of this whole thing. How can a man be pressed on every side? That is not right for a believer. He should know the exceeding greatness of God's power. How can he be perplexed? He must not be with the Lord. He should be hearing the Lord—not perplexed. Why is he pursued by the enemy? Oh dear, it is nothing to do with the gospel. Smitten down! That is not right. No victory! But the interesting thing is that there is another side to it. He said he was pressed on every side, but he was not straightened; he was perplexed, yet not to despair; he was pursued, but he was not forsaken. The Lord was always with him, bringing him out. He was smitten down, but he was not destroyed; always bearing about in the body the dying of Jesus, that the life also of Jesus might be manifested in his mortal flesh.

Then he goes on to say: "For we who live are always delivered unto death for Jesus' sake" (II Corinthians 4:11a). How are you and I delivered unto death? By our beloved friends, by our husbands, by our wives, by our children, by our parents, by our employees, by our employers. God uses multitudinous ways of delivering us unto death. Oh, we don't like it. We say, "Lord, I want to know what it is to be crucified." The Lord says, "I will deliver you unto death." But we want the Lord to come and do it. We want a wonderful experience of seeing the Lord and hearing Him say, "I am delivering you to death." But instead, we see our beloved friends, our beloved relatives, our beloved colleagues at work; and they do not look at all like the Lord. Suddenly, there is an opportunity to die, and we do not like it. We who live are always being delivered unto death for Jesus' sake. Why? That the life also of Jesus might be manifested in these mortal bodies.

Here then, I believe is the key to experiencing and knowing the exceeding greatness of His power to us-ward. It is all to do with the Holy Spirit, His Person, and His work. Don't be afraid of the Holy Spirit.

I am so glad that when I was only seventeen I made a discovery by God Himself. I was at my wits' end. I did not know where to turn or what to do. My whole Christian life seemed to be a facade. I seemed to be singing things, saying things, reading about things, and studying things that were not my experience. In the end, I shut myself up in a little, old, dusty, institutional church building in Woven square in London next to the school of Oriental and African studies. It was like heaven opened and God said to me: "I have given you the Holy Spirit. (It was Jesus.) I have given you the Holy Spirit, yet you do not recognize Him." I actually said to the Lord: "The Holy Spirit! Who is He?" I had been a believer for four years. I was involved in a church that was always talking about Keswick and the Keswick experience, but I had no idea about the Holy Spirit. Then the Lord said to me: "He is in you to reproduce My character and My life, and I will put Him on you and empower you to do My work." I thought it was so wonderful. Heaven opened; and I was so filled with the Lord, I thought I was walking on air. Hours had gone by when I walked out of there; but before I went out, the Lord said to me: "I want you to know that Lance has been crucified on the cross." I have never forgotten the shock of those words, and to this day, I remember what I said to the Lord: "Do you mean I have been doing all this work on him, trying to make him such a good Christian, Christianizing him, making him pray and study the word, and you have crucified him?" And the Lord said, "Yes." It was like a weight rolled off my back. I have never forgotten it.

Then the Lord told me: "No more witnessing." I had been witnessing to people every day. I had adopted Wesley's method. Oh, those poor students in the school of Oriental and African studies! They fled from me every time they saw me. In the corridors, they would vanish out of the way; and in the students' commons room, I always got a place, even if it was packed, because nobody dared to be near me. They knew that before I was with them for very long, I would start on them.

So I said to the Lord: "I don't speak to anyone?"

"No, not to one, not until I tell you."

For three weeks, I never spoke to a soul about their salvation. Isn't that amazing! For the first time in my life, I lived; I actually lived. I enjoyed; I laughed; I became myself. After three weeks, someone came up to me in the commons room and said to me: "There is something different about you. We have been talking about you and saying that there is something different about you. What is it? Three weeks before, I would have said: "I know I have been saved by the grace of God and you are a sinner on your way to hell." But I said to the fellow, who was the leader of the football team, "I really do not know. We are both sinners, and I only know that I have been saved by God." He burst into tears in the middle of the whole commons room, and with tears running down his face, he said, "How can I know the Lord, like you?" Well, I thought, "This must be counterfeit. I have been trying to get someone saved for all these years and nobody has ever gotten saved. Now suddenly, this fellow comes like this." So I just said to him: "You just ask the Lord into your heart."

"How do I do that?"

"You just ask Him into your heart."

"Where do I do it?"

"Well, anywhere."

"Here?"

"Yes, you can do it here."

He bowed his head and said, "Jesus, I do not know who You are, but come into my heart." And the Lord came into his heart. It taught me one thing. For four years, I had tried to get people saved; I had tried to do the work of God;

I had tried to be a Christian, and the whole thing was a laborious burden. It took away all my joy, all my laughter, all my spontaneity. It turned me into some artificial Christian facade. When the Lord showed me that the Holy Spirit was in me and upon me, when He showed me that I had been crucified with Christ, that day was the day when I began to experience the exceeding greatness of His power.

Dear friends, consider what the Lord has made available to you.

4.
Christis the Power of God

Matthew 28:18

And Jesus came to them and spake unto them, saying, All authority hath been given unto me in heaven and on earth

Psalm 110:1–2

[The Lord] saith unto my Lord, Sit thou at my right hand, until I make thine enemies thy footstool. [The Lord] will send forth the rod of thy strength out of Zion: Rule thou in the midst of thine enemies.

Revelation 5:1–14

And I saw in the right hand of him that sat on the throne a book written within and on the back, close sealed with seven seals. And I saw a strong angel proclaiming with a great voice, Who is worthy to open the book, and to loose the seals thereof? And no one in the heaven, or on the earth, or under the earth, was able to open the book, or to look thereon. And I wept much, because no one was found worthy to open the book, or to look thereon: and one of the elders saith unto me, Weep not; behold, the Lion that is of the tribe of Judah, the Root of David, hath overcome to open the book and the seven seals thereof. And I saw in the midst of the throne and of the four living creatures, and in the midst of the elders, a [little] Lamb standing, as though it had been slain, having seven horns, and seven eyes, which are the seven Spirits of God, sent forth into all the earth. And he came, and he taketh it out of the right hand of him that sat on the throne. And when he had taken the book, the four living creatures and the four and twenty elders fell down before the Lamb, having each one a harp, and golden bowls full of incense, which are the prayers of the saints. And they sing a

new song, saying, Worthy art thou to take the book, and to open the seals thereof: for thou wast slain, and didst purchase unto God with thy blood men of every tribe, and tongue, and people, and nation, and madest them to be unto our God a kingdom and priests; and they reign upon the earth.

And I saw, and I heard a voice of many angels round about the throne and the living creatures and the elders; and the number of them was ten thousand times ten thousand, and thousands of thousands; saying with a great voice, Worthy is the Lamb that hath been slain to receive the power, and riches, and wisdom, and might, and honor, and glory, and blessing. And every created thing which is in the heaven, and on the earth, and under the earth, and on the sea, and all

> *things that are in them, heard I saying, Unto him that sitteth on the throne, and unto the Lamb, be the blessing, and the honor, and the glory, and the dominion, for ever and ever. And the four living creatures said, Amen. And the elders fell down and worshipped.*

"For thine is the kingdom, and the power, and the glory, for ever. Amen." At this very moment, all power is in the hands of the Lord Jesus. It is not in the hands of the President of the United States or the Prime Minister of England; it is not in the hands of the President of Russia; it certainly is not in the hands of the United Nations. It is in the hands of the Lord Jesus. After going through the cross and being raised from the dead, He said, "All authority and power is given into My hands, both in heaven and on earth." So it is a most marvellous thing to consider that all the power, the real power, the effective power is in the hands of the One who alone is absolutely worthy to exercise such power.

Psalm 110 is a wonderful Psalm: "The Lord saith unto my Lord, Sit thou at my right hand, until I make thine enemies thy footstool. The Lord will send forth the rod of thy strength out of Zion: Rule thou in the midst of thine enemies." In other words, the Lord Jesus is seated, right now, at the right hand of the Majesty on high; and He is seated till the Father, by the Holy Spirit, makes all the enemies of the Lord Jesus, including antichrist himself, His footstool, the stool for His feet. He is ruling in the midst of His enemies.

In 1 Corinthians 1:23–24, Paul wrote: "But we preach Christ crucified, unto Jews a stumbling block, and unto Gentiles foolishness; but unto them that are called, both Jews and Greeks, Christ the power of God, and the wisdom of God."

I want to give you a bird's-eye view of three tremendous matters that affect the life of every one of us and the life of our fellowship together, and what it reveals is that Christ is the power of God. As we get a glimpse of these matters, we will have to say: "Thine is the power for ever."

The Title Deed of the Universe

The first picture is what we have read in the book of Revelation. It comes after the vision of the risen, glorified, all-powerful Messiah in the midst of the seven churches; He says, "Fear not; I am the first and the last, and the Living one; and I was dead, and behold, I am alive forever more, and I have the keys of death and of Hades [hell]" (Revelation 1:17b–18). It is a marvellous picture.

Then another vision was given to John; and however we interpret this, there are certain things about it that are absolutely marvellous. John saw into heaven itself and he saw, at the heart of everything, the throne of God. On the throne of God, he saw that One sitting, as it were, in unapproachable light. He saw the scroll, but exactly how he saw it we do not know. In the English, it is translated as a book; but in actual fact, it was a scroll. Books were not bound as we have them now in the West. They were scrolls, written on both sides, rolled up, and bound by seven seals. Today, it does not mean a lot to people; but in John's day, any Jew and any one who read what he wrote concerning this vision would have understood it. Title deeds, testaments, or wills were always written very closely on a scroll, bound up tightly, and then sealed with seven seals to insure that if one got broken or tampered with the others would remain intact. You could see very quickly if someone had added something to the will or to the inheritance because all seven seals would have to be broken to do that.

John saw into heaven itself, and at the very heart of everything was the throne of God. Around the throne of God were the four living ones and the twenty-four elders, representing the redeemed from both covenants. Then he saw in the hand of the One on the throne the title deed, this inheritance; and then he heard going through heaven like a clarion call: "Who is worthy to take this scroll and open the seals?" There was absolute silence. Not a soul moved—not in heaven, not on earth, not under the earth. It must have been one of the most pregnant silences that John ever experienced, and so tremendous was the significance of it to John. He at least understood what it meant. He could not help himself; he burst into tears. He was almost beside himself with grief because no one could take that scroll which represented, as it were, the purpose of God—the eternal purpose of God for the universe, God's purpose for mankind, God's purpose for the whole creation. John understood something of the vital importance of it. He was, after all, in a forced labour camp, being worked to death. All around him men were dying, driven to death by their captors. He understood the significance. Oh, when is this old creation, when is this world, when is this universe going to be released from this awful bondage, this wickedness, this tyranny into the liberty of the glory of God?

John was so beside himself that one of the twenty-four elders came up and put his arm around him and said, "Don't cry, don't cry. Look, the Lion who is of the tribe of Judah, the Root of David, has overcome." John looked and saw a little Lamb standing as though it had been slained. What an extraordinary picture! He looked to see this Lion of the tribe of Judah and saw instead a little, almost diminutive Lamb, a year-old Lamb, as if it had been slain, in the midst of the throne. This Lamb took the scroll and began to break open the seals, and the whole of heaven burst into rapturous praise and worship. First it was the four living creatures and the twenty-four elders; then ten thousand times ten thousand, and thousands upon thousands of angels were prostrating themselves before the throne of God. It is unbelievable! And the song is so wonderful, too.

"Thine is the power for ever." It is the Lord Jesus. He has taken the purpose of God for this universe, the purpose of God for this creation, the purpose of God for mankind and secured it. He has realized it. How can I communicate the wonder of it!

"Look, the Lion who is of the tribe of Judah, the Root of David, has overcome." In Genesis 49:10, it was promised that the sceptre would not depart from Judah until He should come, whose right it was to rule. It was not just David; it was David's greater Son. Most believers do not think about the Lion of the tribe of Judah; they only think about the little Lamb, and quite rightly. They put all the emphasis upon the Lamb. But when the elder first spoke to John, he could have said, "Look at the Lamb; see the Lamb of God. Look; the Lamb, He has overcome." He did not say that. He said, "Look, the Lion who is of the tribe of Judah has prevailed and overcome." Most people of Gentile background think of a lion as being strong, magnificent in his strength, as the king of the beasts. When he roars, everybody trembles. That is what they see as the Lion of the tribe of Judah. But this is a title, and what it really means is "the Prince of the Jewish royal house has overcome."

In my family, we have had the name Judah on my father's side in every single generation for nearly 2,000 years. It is only natural when a Jew finds the Lord to get very excited about the Lion of the tribe of Judah. It is Jesus, born King of the Jews, acclaimed King of the Jews, who died with only one title over His head: Jesus of Nazareth, the King of the Jews. He was raised on the third day, and His Messianic Kingship was vindicated and declared by that resurrection. He ascended to the right hand of God as King of Israel, the Messianic King. He is Head of the church, King of kings, and Lord of lords; but He has never abdicated as far as Israel is concerned.

God has a purpose for this old creation. Sometimes, Christians have no time for this creation. They look at this universe and say, "The sooner it goes, the better; the whole thing is a mess." God does not look at it like that. God looks upon this universe and this natural creation as it is in its fallen state, spoiled and ruined by Satan and by sin; but He is going to take it out of the hands of Satan and restore it that there will be, in the end, a new heaven and a new earth wherein dwells righteousness. There is no doubt about it at all! But the fact remains that God is not going to allow Satan to crow for one single moment to be able to say: "Look what I did to Your universe. Look what I did to Your creation. I ruined it; I spoiled it. You could not do anything about it. So You had to throw in Your glove over it and do something altogether new."

In the Messianic prophecy of Isaiah, it says,

*"And there shall come forth a shoot out of the stock of Jesse,
and a branch out of his roots shall bear fruit. (This is the
root of David.) And the Spirit of [the Lord] shall rest upon
him ... And the wolf shall dwell with the lamb, and the
leopard shall lie down with the kid; and the calf and the
young lion and the fatling together; and a little child shall
lead them. And the cow and the bear shall feed; their young
ones shall lie down together; and the lion shall eat straw like
the ox. And the suckling child shall play on the hole of the
asp [cobra], and the weaned child shall put his hand on the
adder's [viper's] den. They shall not hurt nor destroy in all my
holy mountain; for the earth shall be full of the knowledge of
[the Lord], as the waters cover the sea. And it shall come to
pass in that day, that the root of Jesse, that standeth for an
ensign of the peoples, unto him shall the nations seek; and
his resting place shall be glorious" Isaiah 11:1–2a, 6–10*

Right at the beginning of this amazing revelation in this last
great book that brings to a close the whole revelation of God in
the other sixty-five books, we see the Lion of the tribe of Judah,
the root of David overcoming. It is the Lamb of God. He is the
Lamb of God. He takes the title deed for the whole universe, for
mankind, for everything to do with it, and He begins to fulfil it.
He secures it.

It has been said that He breaks the seals and the Kremlin falls
to pieces; He breaks another seal and another thing happens.
People think it is a little bit too fanciful, but it is not so fanciful as

some might think. Actually, all that is happening in our day and generation is exactly that. The only national ecology in the world that has been restored is the national ecology of Israel. Everywhere else, there is damaged ecology. Israel is the only national ecology in the world where desert has been restored to fertility, aridity to forest, barrenness to fruitfulness, people lessness to people everywhere. It is an unbelievable thing how the birds come back. A billion birds go through this little country every year, backwards and forwards. Many of the animals have come back. It is both exciting and amazing. It is not that Israel does not have problems with pollution of water, pollution of air; but the fact is, it is the only national ecology in the world that has been restored. Why? It is because the King is coming back to Jerusalem and the whole ecology of the world is going to be restored. There is no one else who can sew up the hole in the ozone layer over America and the Antarctic. There is no one else who can do anything about the pollution of the seas. Most scientists feel it has gone too far now. Only the Lord Jesus can do it.

I remember once having a discussion about the four living creatures with Mr. Sparks, and he said he believed that in some way they represented the whole natural creation. We do not usually think of that; we only think about human beings. We do not realize God has a natural creation. The Lord Jesus put it like this, and it was not sentimentally; He meant it: "Are not two sparrows sold for a farthing? and not one of them falls to the ground without your Father" (see Matthew 10:29). It is the most amazing statement.

What does it all mean? It means that, somehow or other, there is coming a day when something is going to happen to this old universe, when God gets what He wants in man, when He actually reaches that point He has been driving toward all the way through. It will never be the power of man; it will never be, even, the power of Christians; it will never be the power of servants of the Lord. It is His power and His power alone that will bring it into being. He is the heart of the whole matter. It is Christ crucified, the power of God. Oh, how wonderful that is!

I have often thought of these amazing things in the Scripture where it talks about trees clapping their hands, hills and valleys singing for joy. What does it mean, unless somehow, at some point, God is going to do something and put right all that sin has put wrong in this universe? He can only do that when He has the Lord Jesus at the heart of the whole thing—and those whom the Lord Jesus has redeemed.

In Romans 8, it speaks of the whole natural creation being subjected to a cycle of futility. I do not even know what it really means. What will happen to a tree when it is no longer subjected to the cycle of corruption and futility? What will happen to plants? What will happen to animals and birds? I have no idea; nor do I think it is good to speculate. Praise the Lord, He has not given us revelation on that; otherwise, we would have a few more denominations. I think it is an amazing thing that whenever we begin to consider this, something leaps within us, even when we do not understand it. Something within us witnesses to it. "It is right," something tells us inside.

How amazing it is when we see this window, as it were, into the heart of everything, and there we see on the throne of the universe, on the very throne of the Lord God Almighty, the Lion of the tribe of Judah, the Lamb of God. Do not think that it is a political accident that God has brought back the Jewish people from the ends of the earth to that little bit of territory He promised them. He made a covenant with our forefathers 4,000 years ago, an unconditional covenant concerning territory, and it is still operative 4,000 years later. God said, "I make this covenant with you and with your seed after you throughout your generations." While there is a physical seed of Abraham through Isaac and through Jacob on the earth, this covenant is operative. God said, "I covenant not only that this land shall be yours for an everlasting inheritance, but I will be your God." The amazing thing about this covenant is that there is no condition. It is unconditional; it is of grace. And God has kept it. The very exiles are actually the evidence that God is keeping the covenant, and the returns are just as great or even more so.

There is another covenant called the Davidic covenant. This Davidic covenant is also absolute. God said, "Of your seed, there shall never fail a man to sit upon your throne forever." God made a covenant with David, so that when David was dying, he actually spoke of the Messiah. His last words were all to do with the Lord Jesus. He said, "God has made a covenant with me, settled and sure."

Isaiah spoke of it, for he said concerning the Lord Jesus: "For unto us a child is born, unto us a son is given; and the government shall be upon his shoulder: and his name shall be called Wonderful, Counsellor, Mighty God, Everlasting Father, Prince of Peace. Of the increase of his government and of peace there shall no end, upon the throne of David, and upon his kingdom" (Isaiah 9:6–7a). You cannot spiritualize this altogether away. You cannot just say it is all over; it makes nonsense of the word of God. The fact of the matter is that by the grace of God you have been brought into the heart of God. You have been brought into the salvation of God. You, also, have been made partakers in this whole thing; you have been made fellow members, fellow heirs, fellow partakers. When that day comes, you will see the King in Jerusalem and the law of God going out from Zion and the word of the Lord from Jerusalem. All the nations will go up to Jerusalem and they will say, "Let us beat our swords into ploughshares and our spears into pruning-hooks; we will learn the art of war no more." What a day! At the heart of this whole thing is the King. It is the Lord Jesus, the Lamb of God, the Lion of the tribe of Judah.

Some of the greatest miracles ahead of us are going to be the salvation of the Jewish people and the work of the gospel going out into all the earth in these days of tremendous shaking and tremendous problems. Here is God's purpose for the universe realized, and it is realized by the Lord Jesus. We can only say, "Thine is the power."

The Spirit of Babylon is Destroyed

Then I think of another window that takes us to Daniel. You remember that great Babylonian Emperor, Nebuchadnezzar, had a dream and he would not tell the wise men what the dream was. He said, "If you are so wise, you tell me what it is." Then he threatened them that if they did not tell him, he would have their heads off. That really put the fear of God in them all. They found Daniel and asked him if he would seek his God; and God gave Daniel the understanding. It was an unbelievable dream. Nebuchadnezzar actually saw the whole history of fallen man's civilization.

It was, in fact, in four great kingdoms—the Babylonians succeeded by the Persians succeeded by the Hellenists or Greeks succeeded by the Romans, and then coming right down to our own day, to modern civilization. The head, which was gold, was Babylon; but actually, the whole thing was Babylon. It is the spirit of Babylon and the character of Babylon: "Let us make a name for ourselves; let us build a tower that will reach to heaven lest we be scattered abroad on the face of the earth." You have here an amazing spiritual insight into the heart of fallen human history. Although we have only these four great empires—which are the root of our modern civilization, the progenitor or procreator of it—actually, every great civilization in the world, including the Chinese, including the Inca, including the Indian, is in this thing. It is there in spirit. It is not mentioned, but it is there in spirit because this is man's city; this is man's kingdom. It is the kingdom of man, the power of man, and the glory of man. It is man's civilization, man's creative genius, man's energy, man's talents, man's power.

Isn't it interesting that even though Daniel was uncompromising, he was very diplomatic? He could have said a few other things, but he never did. He could have said to Nebuchadnezzar that it was an idol, which would have been absolutely right. That is exactly what he saw—a huge monolith, an image, an idol. Interestingly, Nebuchadnezzar set up an image just after that and said everyone had to worship it. That is the heart and character of fallen man's civilization. It is self-worship; it is the worship of man, the worship of man's glory, the worship of man's power. Then there is another thing that Daniel could have said, but he was too diplomatic to say it. I have no doubt that Daniel talked it over with Shadrach, Meshach, and Abednego. He could have said, "It has no heart. It is a statue without a heart; a great colossus, perfect in some ways, but it has no heart. It cannot breathe; it cannot move." Later on, Daniel himself had a dream, a vision. He saw the same thing all over again, only he saw it as four wild beasts, ferocious and untameable. They were magnificent, but they were ferocious, untameable beasts—unpredictable. God revealed to Daniel that this is the heart of fallen man's civilization. Even with all the talk about equality and prosperity and peace, the real heart of it is a ferocious, unpredictable, wild beast. And we have seen it all through human history.

When John was on the isle of Patmos, he had a vision, and he saw the same thing again. In both the dream of Nebuchadnezzar and the vision of Daniel, something was not emphasized so much as it was inferred and implied; but when we come to John's vision in Revelation 13, what is emphasized is that the whole thing, somehow, is going to come back with an enormous power at the end of world history, and this time it is going to be universal. The whole world will go after this thing. It says that the false prophet will set up an image and will cause the image to speak and all the nations will worship it.

While Nebuchadnezzar was having this dream, suddenly he saw a stone not made with hands, hurtling, as it were, out of the air, striking the whole great colossus at its weakest point, at its feet. The whole thing shattered in a few moments. Isn't that wonderful! This was a stone not made with hands, meaning that it was not a rock, as some people imagine, the kind of rocks that are thrown around in my part of the world. It says a stone, but not made with hands. In other words, it was a cut stone. Who is that cut stone?

We know who it is. "The stone which the builders disallowed has become the chief corner stone" (see Psalm 118:22). In 1 Peter 2:4–5a, it says, "Unto whom coming, a living stone, rejected indeed of men, but with God elect, precious, ye also, as living stones, are built up a spiritual house." Who is that stone? It is the Lord Jesus. Think of the power God has put into the Lord Jesus, that is expressed in Him. There is that huge, great colossus; and this cut stone hits it and the whole thing is shattered in a moment. That is the power of God. I praise the Lord Jesus. He has said that in the teeth of all the antagonism and all the satanic forces and power and a demonized world, all power is given into His hands, both in heaven and on earth. We can say from the heart: "Thine is the power."

This is not some fairy story. It is not like Hans Christian Andersen's fairy stories or Grimm's fairy stories, which are very lovely, very interesting, very vivid but have nothing to do with us. We are living in this. We are the witnesses of something happening in our own day in world society that has not happened from the very beginning. The only other time anything was muted which would have been world-wide or universal was in Babylonian times, when it seemed as if it was going to cover the whole known earth, or the Persian Empire or the Hellenistic Empire or the Roman Empire. But don't think it is a fairy story. Behind the scenes, there are tremendous moves afoot to give teeth to the United Nations; and the fact is that, for the first time ever, sanctions were put on Iraq, then on Libya, and then on Serbia. It is the first time ever in history, other than South Africa, that such sanctions have been applied, which means that without our even knowing it, a huge new force is arising and we do not even recognize it. For the first time, the world is united to go against a nation in the Middle East (Iraq) and do something with it. It is extraordinary. It has never happened before. As you well know, the first shot that is fired, the United Nations disappears. They are not allowed to stay once there are actual shots or violence or fighting. But now in Serbia, they have sent a thousand Canadian troops and a whole battalion of French Commandos; so we begin to see something happening that is unbelievable. Apart from that, we see a huge new superpower arising on the ashes of the ancient Roman Empire. It is much bigger than that— 361 million people in the greatest bloc of nations in the world. This means a new world order is coming, a new world government is coming, and somehow or other, the North American continent is going to be involved and so is Asia. The whole world is going to be involved in this thing, and it is all in the Book. Praise God, the Lord Jesus has power over it.

When that antichrist appears (and may we not be here to see him), our Lord Jesus, finally, will come and with the breath of His mouth slay him and bring to naught his power by the manifestation of His coming. Power! Don't be afraid. Let them all do their war dances; let the demonized forces and principalities take over if they want to. The Lord Jesus has them on a chain. They can only do what they are allowed to do—no more. When God's time is come, the word will go forth and the whole thing will be ended in a moment. Praise God!

This kingdom appeared in the Roman Empire. Jesus was born in Bethlehem in the Roman Empire just a few years after it had risen. His great work on the cross was done under Roman authority. Isn't it amazing that a representative of Rome was the one who signed His death warrant, and He was crucified in the Roman way? Our Lord Jesus arose from the dead under Roman authority, and He ascended to the right hand of God under Roman authority. They could not stop Him. He went right through them and beyond them, and the most wonderful thing is this: They had no power over Him, nor over the kingdom that He came to bring in. For on that day of Pentecost when He poured out the promise of the Father, the Holy Spirit brought, in actual power, the kingdom of God into our beings. Then for the first time, the throne of God was manifest through believers. Before, it had only been manifest in the Lord Jesus. Then it was manifest through the Lord Jesus as Head and through the members of His body. It turned the Roman world upside down. Praise God!

The second coming of the Lord Jesus is going to take place in the end of this Roman Empire. This whole modern civilization has come out of the Babylonian Empire, out of the Persian Empire, out of the Hellenistic Empire, and out of the Roman Empire. Those dear saints did not see that it was two movements. They only saw it as one; but the wonderful thing is that the Lord Jesus is going to come back again, and when He appears, the whole thing will be shattered. In a moment, it will fall to pieces. Then will come the wonderful cry in Revelation 11:15: "The kingdom of the world is become the kingdom of our Lord, and of his Christ: and he shall reign for ever and ever." Praise the Lord!

The Bride of Christ

There is one other window I want to give you, just as wonderful as the others. In Revelation 21, it speaks of the wife of the Lamb, the new Jerusalem coming down out of heaven, having the glory of God. The Lord Jesus said, "Behold, I make all things new... I am the Alpha and the Omega, the beginning and the end" (see Revelation 21:5–6). This little window is all to do with the bride of Christ, the wife of the Lamb. The Bible begins with a marriage and it ends with a marriage. In the first chapters of Genesis, you have the story of the first man and woman and a marriage; and when you come to Revelation 21, you have another marriage. So the Bible begins and ends with a marriage. The first marriage is human, earthly, transient; the last marriage is spiritual, heavenly, eternal. Then there is something else wonderful. If you take your Bible and open it, more or less, in the centre, you come to two little, tiny books. One is called Ecclesiastes, that many Christians never read, and the other is called the Song of Songs. I think these two marvellous books belong together, because everywhere in Ecclesiastes there is the same refrain: "Vanity, vanity, all is vanity." According to Jewish tradition, it is Solomon, and he tried everything. He built parks; he created zoos; he wrote encyclopaedias; he did a thousand and one things. He certainly knew something about marriage because he had 800 wives. The whole of Ecclesiastes has to do with human life, human knowledge, and he says at the end of it: "All is vanity, vanity; all is vanity." Let me put it another way: "Emptiness, emptiness; all is emptiness." Let me put it another way: "Stupidity, stupidity; all is stupidity."

Solomon says, "What does it matter what you do? Here is a good man and he dies young. Here is an evil man and he dies old. You work all day and you get nothing for it. It is stupidity; it is vanity." Many people have questioned why Ecclesiastes is in the Bible. It does not seem to be very Christian or very spiritual. Yet it is absolutely necessary because unless you and I know the Lord, then everything is stupidity. All the empires you build, you leave. You came into the world naked, you go out naked. You can build a huge business empire and you leave it in the end. You can do a thousand and one things but you leave it in the end.

When we come to the Song of Songs, which according to Jewish tradition was a revelation given to Solomon of the love between God and His people, then we suddenly find that the whole purpose of our being created is to do with a love story. God actually loves us, and He loves us so much that He wants us. Why, we shall never know; but He wants us. The story is how, first, He comes to this dear one and reveals Himself. She gets excited and then she becomes very familiar with Him. She decides that He loves her and that is all that matters. It is very interesting how she put it: "He is mine and I am His." It is "mine," and that is the point. So the Lord leaves her, and later, after dealings, she finds Him again. She has been disciplined in some way, and now she has a different refrain. "I am His and He is mine." But then He deals with her even further, and the last refrain is so beautiful: "I am His." The "mine" has gone out of it. Isn't it interesting that there is a marriage at the beginning of the Bible, a marriage at the end of the Bible, and a marriage at the centre of the Bible?

John the Baptist spoke of himself as the best man. He said, "I am the best man at the wedding; I am the bridegroom's friend."

The Apostle Paul said in Ephesians 5 that Jesus sought for a bride that He might present her to Himself a glorious church, not having spot or wrinkle or any such thing. As we get older, we know all about spots and wrinkles and such things. What a wonderful thing that the Lord deals with all these things.

The Lord Jesus put it another way: "Upon this rock, I will build My church; and the gates of hell shall not prevail against it" (see Matthew 16:18). He never said, "Upon this rock, I will build My church until the last days and then I will give it up; it will be too impossible." No; He said, "Upon this rock, I will build My church," and He actually mentioned the gates of hell—that they would not prevail against it. So we suddenly discover that in the heart of the Lord Jesus there is a determination, a passion to prepare a people for Himself, to build the church.

When we come to the book of Revelation, we see all the martyrdom, the great world-wide antichrist system; we see dragons, serpents, beasts, and all the rest of it. It seems so all-powerful, universal, invincible, immovable. Some people are afraid to read the book of Revelation for this very reason. But then we come to that wonderful word: "Hallelujah: for the Lord our God, the Almighty reigneth. Let us rejoice and be exceeding glad, and let us give the glory unto him: for the marriage of the Lamb is come, and his [bride] hath made herself ready" (Revelation 19:6b–7). The Lord has done it! He has done it in spite of 2,000 years of church history in which we Christians have frustrated every move of the Holy Spirit; in which we have taken everything that the Holy Spirit has created from the throne of God in what I would call almost mini-Pentecosts and then institutionalized them, traditionalized them, crystallized them, systematized them, and killed such a movement of the Spirit. Now we have all around us in Christendom monuments to works of the Holy Spirit in past generations.

I am not saying that God is not still at work in ancient denominational churches or in the institutions. It is amazing where you find the Lord; it is wonderful where you find the Lord. It is really amazing. But the fact still remains of what we have done. As Golda Meir once said: "When we have friends like some of our friends, we don't need enemies." Some of the friends of the Lord do more damage to the purpose of God than the enemy himself. But in spite of 2,000 years of church history in which we have frustrated every move that God has made by His Spirit to recover that church, He is going to do it. We have got it in the Book. Finally, the bride will make herself ready, not in some universal move that will include every single believer but in some marvellous work of His Spirit. I believe we have partly witnessed this in our own day; it is by the awakening of millions and millions of real believers to the purpose of God, to the heart of God, to the passion of the Lord Jesus.

How wonderful it is that in the very last chapter of the Bible, it says, "The Spirit and the bride say, 'Come'." Can you imagine how overjoyed the Holy Spirit will be when finally He has the bride? It has been His work all the way through to produce this bride; and now, finally, here she is and the Spirit and the bride say, "Come." I think we can only say one thing: "Thine is the power for ever."

Mount up with Wings as Eagles

There is one last word and it is a personal word that I want to communicate to you. I am quite sure that the Lord gave me this word and I am quite sure it is for many people here. I do not know what is in store for us in the future, but I have no doubt that the Lord gave me this little word. These days we are living in are invigorating, in one sense. They are so exciting, so invigorating because we see with our own eyes things being fulfilled. Any person who has got anything spiritual in them at all has to be invigorated. You must be more than half dead if you are just fearful of what you see. Dead fish "swim" with the current; live fish use the current and swim against it. I think what we see is very invigorating, inspiring, and encouraging; but it is also exhausting. Everywhere I go, I find the Lord's people, especially servants of God, exhausted. It is almost as if, unbeknown to us, a new pressure has come into the atmosphere. Out in the front lines, you have always felt the pressure and tension and the power of the enemy around you. In the so-called Christian homelands, somehow or other, much of Satan's work has been bound, to a certain extent, by the work of the gospel. But no more; it is truly the post-Christian era. Satan is bent on seeing that those areas that saw the greatest revivals and greatest awakenings will become the greatest hell pits in the last part of world history.

In Daniel 7:25, it speaks about the antichrist wearing out the saints. In Revelation 12, it speaks about Satan coming down, knowing that his time is short. In another place it speaks of great foul spirits like frogs going out over the whole earth. It speaks of the Lord giving the saints over to the powers of darkness for a period. Now I am not saying that we are in that period now, but as we move toward it, you can begin to feel the pressure upon family life, upon relationships within marriages, upon relationships in Christian work, upon relationships in the church. You begin to feel it personally even as individuals. Our Lord Jesus Himself said that men's hearts will faint for fear and expectation of those things coming upon the face of the earth, because the powers of the heavens shall be shaken. Now we have not got there yet; but He said when you see these things begin to come to pass, look up, lift up your heads because your redemption draweth nigh.

In Isaiah 40:27–30, it says, "Why saith thou, O Jacob, and speakest, O Israel, My way is hid from [the Lord], and the justice due to me is passed away from my God? Hast thou not known? hast thou not heard? The everlasting God, [the Lord], the Creator of the ends of the earth, fainteth not, neither is weary; there is no searching of his understanding. He giveth power to the faint; and to him that hath no might he increaseth strength. Even the youths shall faint and be weary, and the young men shall utterly fall: but they that wait for [the Lord] shall renew their strength; they shall mount up with wings as eagles; they shall run, and not be weary; they shall walk, and not faint."

We have said all the way through: "Thine is the power for ever." All power belongs to God, and that is exactly what it says here; but the way this puts it is even more wonderful. "He giveth power to the faint; and to him that hath no might he increases strength." Do you qualify? If you think you have power, you do not qualify. If you think you have strength and might of your own, you do not qualify. But if you feel faint, he gives power to the faint; and if you feel you have no might, he increases strength. I think it is so marvellous. Here we have a wonderful promise of never tiring, unfainting, unfading power of God. It is at your disposal. Will you please note the promise that He shall renew your strength? We need that. We need our strength to be renewed. We are never going to go through these days without the Lord. But the Lord says He will renew our strength.

Then it says, "They shall mount up with wings as eagles; they shall run, and not be weary; they shall walk, and not faint." Why didn't the Lord put it the other way around? It would be natural to say, "They shall walk and not faint, they shall run and not be weary, they shall mount up with wings as eagles." You have the picture of someone on a runway—walking and not fainting, getting into a run and not getting weary, and finally taking off. No; the Lord did not say that because what the Lord really wants is that we should mount up with wings as eagles. But if we cannot do that, we can run and not be weary; and if we cannot do that, we can walk and not faint.

Now I am a lazy person, so I think to myself: If I walk, I have to use my legs; if I run, I have to use my legs and my lungs. It is much better to fly. When you learn to fly, you use the air currents. If you have ever seen eagles, you may know that they are the most extraordinary creatures. I am always telling my cockatoos and parrots I wish they were eagles. Eagles are such extraordinary creatures. Not only do they use thermal air currents, they even use the storm. They are not afraid. There is something majestic and powerful about the eagle. Yet when you see, as sometimes we do in my part of the world, a huge storm, a powerful storm with the lightning and the thunder bolts— and there is the eagle. It is extraordinary! When the Lord says,

"They shall mount up with wings as eagles," He is saying that He will create in you a capacity and enable you to use the storms of life and the currents of life—things that should destroy you— to fulfil your ministry, to fulfil your work, that the purpose of God might be fulfilled in you.

Have we not reached the place as those who know and love the Lord where youth are fainting and young men are utterly failing? We associate youth and we associate young men with strength, with athletic strength, with muscular strength. But it says there will come a day when the youth will faint and the young men will utterly fail, but those that wait for the Lord shall renew their strength. Waiting for the Lord is even more than waiting on the Lord. Waiting on the Lord is a key to so much, but to wait for the Lord is the mark of true spiritual character. You never wait for the Lord until your natural power is ended, until your natural strength is finished; then you learn to wait on and to wait for the Lord. But if you learn to wait for the Lord, you will renew your strength and you will mount up with wings as eagles. You will run the course and not be weary; you will walk the walk of faith and not faint.

May the Lord do it; and if by His grace He does it for us, what will be our response? I think our response can be only one: "Thine is the power for ever. Amen."

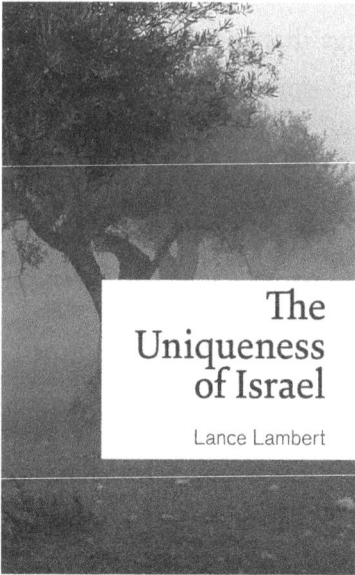

The Uniqueness of Israel

Woven into the fabric of Jewish existence there is an undeniable uniqueness. There is bitter controversy over the subject of Israel, but time itself will establish the truth about this nation's place in God's plan. For Lance Lambert, the Lord Jesus is the key that unlocks Jewish history He is the key not only to their fall, but also to their restoration. For in spite of the fact that they rejected Him, He has not rejected them.

Till The Day Dawns

Lance Lambert

Till the Day Dawns

"And we have the word of prophecy made more sure; whereunto ye do well that ye take heed, as unto a lamp shining in a dark place, until the day dawn, and the day-star arise in your hearts." (II Peter 1:9).

The word of prophecy was not given that we might merely be comforted but that we would be prepared and made ready. Let us look into the Word of God together, searching out the prophecies, that the Day-Star arise in our hearts until the Day dawns.

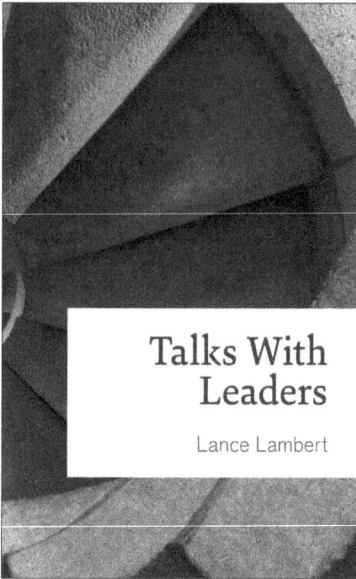

Talks With Leaders

"O Timothy, guard that which is committed unto thee ..."
(1 Timothy 6:20) Has God given you something? Has God
deposited something in you? Is there something of Himself
which He has given to you to contribute to the people of God?
Guard it. Guard that vision which He has given you. Guard that
understanding that He has so mercifully granted to you. Guard
that experience which He has given that it does not evaporate or
drain away or become a cause of pride. Guard that which the Lord
has given to you by the Holy Spirit. In these heart-to-heart talks
with leaders Lance Lambert covers such topics as the character
of God's servants, the way to serve, the importance of anointing,
and hearing God's voice. Let us consider together how to remain
faithful with what has been entrusted to us.

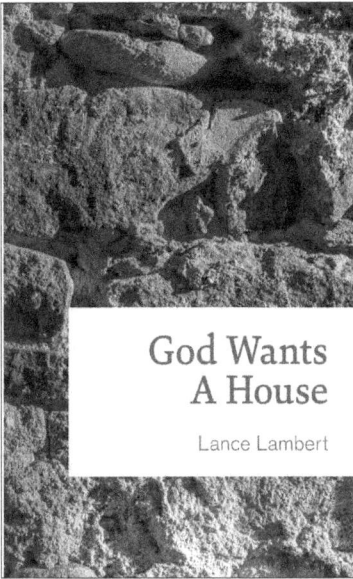

God Wants a House

Where is God at home? Is He at home in Richmond, VA? Is He at home in Washington? Is He at home in Richmond, Surrey? Is He at home in these other places? Where is God at home? There are thousands of living stones, many, many dear believers with real experience of the Lord, but where has the ark come home? Where are the staves being lengthened that God has finally come home? In God Wants a House Lance looks into this desire of the Lord, this desire He has to dwell with His people. What would this dwelling look like? Let's seek the Lord, that we can say with David, "One thing have I asked of Jehovah, that will I seek after: that I may dwell in the house of Jehovah all the days of my life, To behold the beauty of Jehovah, And to inquire in his temple."

www.ingramcontent.com/pod-product-compliance
Lightning Source LLC
Chambersburg PA
CBHW061149040426
42445CB00013B/1627